The Adventures of the Chickpea and the Rise of the Pearl of Wisdom

Shah Pezeshk

Published by

Dedicatory Note

Dedicated to the Loving Memory of My Brother, Shahabeddin Pezeshkzad

From my earliest childhood memories, my brother was my first storyteller.

I can still see him holding the black hardcover book, filled with illustrated tales, carefully turning each page, bringing the stories to life with his voice, his warmth, and his love.

He was not only a brother—he was a mentor, a guide, and a source of unwavering encouragement.

He nurtured my love for storytelling, reminding me that stories have the power to inspire, uplift, and transform lives.

As a pioneer, a teacher, and a devoted servant of the Faith, he carried a profound wisdom and a boundless spirit of service—values that shaped my journey as a writer and as a seeker of truth.

This book is dedicated to him, with deep gratitude for his love, wisdom, and belief in my voice.

May his soul continue its glorious ascent in the realms of eternity,

and may his light forever shine in the hearts of those who were blessed to know him.

Shahrokh Pezeshk

TABLE OF CONTENTS

DEDICATORY NOTE	I
PREFACE	1
INTRODUCTION: THE RISE OF NOKHODEE—A CHICKPEA'S JOURNEY OF WONDER	4
CHAPTER ONE: THE HUMBLE BEGINNING—A PRAYER, A WISH, AND A CHICKPEA	8
CHAPTER TWO: A CHICKPEA WITH A PURPOSE	11
CHAPTER THREE (PART 1): THE INVENTOR BEHIND THE GARAGE	15
CHAPTER THREE (PART 2): THE HARSH JOURNEY—FACING TRIALS ON DRY LAND	17
CHAPTER FOUR: THE FIVE STAGES OF TRANSFORMATION	48
CHAPTER FIVE: THE CALL OF THE OCEAN	55
CHAPTER SIX: THE LEAP OF FAITH—JUMPING INTO THE WATERS	68
CHAPTER SEVEN: THE KOI FISH AND THE DOLPHIN—LESSONS OF TRANSFORMATION	74
CHAPTER EIGHT: THE PEARL MAKER'S SECRET—INSIDE THE OYSTER	80
CHAPTER NINE: THE RETURN TO THE SURFACE—A NEW MISSION BEGINS	86
CHAPTER TEN: THE FIRST CHALLENGE—BREAKING THE ILLUSIONS OF WEALTH	90
CHAPTER ELEVEN: THE RESISTANCE—WHEN THE POWERFUL REFUSE TO CHANGE	95

CHAPTER TWELVE: THE AWAKENING—BRINGING TRUTH TO THE PEOPLE   **99**

CHAPTER THIRTEEN: THE CLASH—THE BATTLE FOR THE FUTURE BEGINS   **111**

CHAPTER FOURTEEN: THE FALL OF THE TOWER—A NEW ERA BEGINS   **116**

EPILOGUE: THE JOURNEY CONTINUES   **124**

A FINAL THOUGHT   **136**

THE FINAL MESSAGE: TRANSFORMATION IS FOR THE WORLD   **138**

ABOUT THE AUTHOR   **139**

PREFACE

The Grain and the Pearl: A Friendship that Illuminates

It was one of those afternoons — the kind where time seems to hang suspended, inviting a deep dive into the soul of things. On just such an afternoon, I first encountered *The Adventures of the Chickpea and the Rise of the Pearl of Wisdom*. Fresh from the press, the book exuded a unique fragrance — a blend of fresh ink and timeless promises — as though each page safeguarded a secret whispered by the winds of time. I must confess, it took only a few lines to recognise the soul pulsing behind those words: Shah Pezeshk, my friend of decades, the storyteller who has always had the gift of transforming the ordinary into the extraordinary.

Some books arrive quietly, almost as if politely seeking permission to enter our lives. Others, like this one, burst in like a gale, announcing that the hour of transformation has arrived. With each page turned, I was carried away on a tide of emotions, like a chickpea cast upon ocean waves, heading towards a horizon where fantasy and reality intertwine in a mesmerising dance. Who would have thought that a simple grain, so small and seemingly insignificant, could carry within it the seed of such a grand dream — the driving force to change the world?

Nokhodee, the unlikely hero of this saga, quickly won me over with his determination and insatiable thirst for knowledge. In his journey, I recognised the hopes and fears that live in every human heart: the desire to break free from imposed limitations, to transcend the mundane, to leave an indelible mark on history. And, like the chickpea, I too felt compelled to question my own place in the world, to rethink my choices, and to re-evaluate my values.

With narrative mastery, Shah weaves a plot rich in symbolism and metaphor, inviting readers to uncover the multiple meanings hidden within each character, each setting, and each event. The Man of Crystal Glass, the Phoenix of Love, the Blue Butterfly… each of them represents virtues and qualities that inspire us to become better versions of ourselves, cultivating wisdom, resilience, and compassion. Together, they reveal that true strength lies in unity, in collaboration, and in our capacity to build a fairer, more equal world.

What enchants me most about Shah's writing is his effortless movement between past and present, tradition and modernity. In *The Adventures of the Chickpea*, ancestral elements such as the teachings of the Bahá'í Faith are beautifully harmonised with cutting-edge technologies like drones and artificial intelligence, creating a narrative that is both timeless and contemporary. In doing so, the author reminds us that the search for meaning is a constant throughout human history — a challenge renewed by every generation.

Yet beyond its aesthetic beauty and philosophical richness, this book touched me on a very personal level. Throughout the reading, I felt that Shah was not merely telling a story but inviting me to embark on a journey of self-discovery, to dive into the depths of my own being in search of the sleeping pearl. And in doing so, he reminded me that true transformation is not instantaneous, but the result of a continuous process of learning, reflection, and surrender.

That is why, upon reaching the final page, I felt deep gratitude for the privilege of having read this book. And it is why I am honoured to write this preface — not as a literary critic, but as a friend eager to share with the world the beauty and wisdom of this remarkable work. May *The Adventures of the Chickpea and the Rise of the Pearl of Wisdom* inspire many readers to find their own voice, to embrace their dreams, and to become agents of transformation within their own worlds. After all, as Shah Pezeshk teaches us, true magic lies in the courage to dream, to serve, and to transform.

Washington Araújo

Writer, journalist, and holder of a Master's degree in Film

Introduction: The Rise of Nokhodee—A Chickpea's Journey of Wonder

This book is designed for children and young adults, or anyone wanting to explore their inner child, combining adventure with wisdom. Every great story begins with a small seed—sometimes quite literally. The story of Nokhodee, the little chickpea, was born from memories of my childhood in Tehran, where storytelling was more than just entertainment—it was a bridge between generations, a source of wonder, and a way to connect with the world beyond our rooftops.

I would also like to acknowledge that using AI as a tool has helped me write this book. Also, my upbringing in a country where the very basics of my belief system were constantly challenged helped me to uphold a set of new universal principles and beliefs shared in this book, inspired by my belief in the Bahá'í Faith.

As a child, I spent many summer nights on the flat rooftops of our home, where families gathered to escape the heat of the city. The sky stretched endlessly above us, dotted with stars, and the air carried the faint scent of jasmine. It was there, under the vast Persian night, that my storytelling journey truly began. My younger brother was my first listener, but soon, other children from neighbouring homes started hopping over the low walls that separated our rooftops. Their eager faces and wide-eyed curiosity made me realise the power of storytelling—how a well-told tale could transport young minds beyond the limits of their everyday world.

But the roots of Nokhodee's story go deeper, intertwined with the simple, everyday wisdom of my grandmother. Every morning before school, she would hand me a small pouch of *Nokhodchee va Keshmesh*—a mix of roasted chickpeas and raisins. It was her way of keeping us healthy and away from sweets, though at the time, I thought little of it. It was only later that I saw something remarkable in those tiny chickpeas. They were small but packed with energy, modest yet essential, overlooked yet nourishing—much like so many people in this world whose true potential goes unnoticed.

One day, the thought struck me: What if a humble chickpea could dream? What if it refused to accept its fate of simply being eaten? What if it aspired to do something greater—to grow, to explore, to change the world? That was the moment Nokhodee was born—not just as a character, but as a reflection of all those who dare to dream beyond their limitations.

The story of Nokhodee is deeply personal, inspired by my own childhood experiences and the lessons I learned growing up in Tehran—the power of perseverance, the beauty of transformation, and the idea that even the smallest among us can rise to greatness. Just as I once captivated children on the rooftops with my stories, I now invite you to embark on this journey—one that begins with a simple chickpea but unfolds into an adventure filled with wisdom, resilience, and the limitless potential that lies within us all.

From the humble farmhouse where his story began, Nokhodee embarks on an extraordinary journey of transformation, gathering a diverse team of companions, each with a unique role to play. Guided by wisdom, resilience, and faith, they navigate trials that test their courage and purpose—from treacherous landscapes and hidden dangers to the depths of the ocean, where Nokhodee undergoes a profound metamorphosis. Emerging as the Pearl of Wisdom, he carries not only the lessons of his journey but also a newfound mission: to share his knowledge and the mystery of true prosperity with the world.

Upon returning to the surface, the Pearl of Wisdom and his companions confront the harsh realities of economic disparity and systemic greed. He and his companions venture into the heart of the City of Gold and Shadows, where wealth and suffering exist side by side, as they challenge the powerful figures who control the world's economy. Their message is simple yet revolutionary—true prosperity lies not in hoarding wealth by some, but in service, unity, and sustainable growth available to all.

While some leaders resist, the Pearl of Wisdom's call for change begins to stir a transformation among the people. With the help of his allies—the Phoenix of Love, the Crystal Glass Man, and later others who step in—the Australian Shepherd, the Dragonfly, and the

American Eagle, the movement for justice gains momentum, revealing hidden truths and inspiring a shift in global consciousness.

As the battle for the future unfolds, the book explores the deeper meaning of wealth, the illusions of power, and the role of wisdom in shaping a just and equitable world. It is a story of faith, perseverance, and the unyielding spirit of those who seek truth beyond material gain—a faith inspired by the teachings of all great Manifestations of God, including Christ, Buddha, Moses, Krishna, Mohammed, and Bahá'u'lláh.

More than a tale of adventure, it is an allegory for personal and societal transformation, inviting readers—young and old—to reflect on their own purpose and the legacy they wish to leave behind. Suggestions for points of discussion are provided at the end of each chapter, in the form of specific titles for key points in the story, namely the final chapter: *The Power of Timing*, *A Moment of Surrender*, and *The Beginning of a New Era*, to help the reader transition emotionally and intellectually between the scenes.

Through the journey of a simple chickpea—who transforms into a Pearl of Wisdom—the book offers a vision of hope: a world where knowledge, love, and justice, resulting in unity and peace, illuminate the path to a brighter future.

Welcome to the story of Nokhodee, the little chickpea. Welcome to a world where even the smallest seed can change the world.

Chapter One: The Humble Beginning—A Prayer, a Wish, and a Chickpea

The golden fields swayed gently under the warm afternoon sun, stretching as far as the eye could see. Inside a small farmhouse at the edge of the fields, a husband and wife sat together, their voices low, their hands clasped.

"We have prayed for so many years," the husband sighed, "and yet, no child has come to bless our home despite our prayers."

His wife smiled softly, placing a hand on his. "Perhaps our prayers have already been answered in ways we cannot yet see."

The man looked at her, puzzled. "How do you mean?"

"Sometimes," she said, "we look for something grand, something obvious. But what if our blessing is waiting for us in an unexpected way?"

The husband thought for a moment before shaking his head. "Maybe you're right. But what I know for sure is that I'm hungry. Let me gather some ingredients from the farm so we can cook a meal."

His wife chuckled. "Go on, then. Pick something fresh."

So off he went, stepping out into the golden waves of chickpeas. He ran his hands through the plants, letting the pods brush against his fingers.

"Hmm… this one looks good," he muttered, reaching down to pluck a chickpea pod.

But just as he was about to take it, a tiny voice whispered through the wind.

"Please, don't pick me just yet!"

The farmer blinked, looking around. "Who said that?"

He bent down and stared at the little chickpea inside its pod, resting among thousands of others.

"It was me," the chickpea whispered again. "I have a dream!"

The farmer chuckled, shaking his head. "A talking chickpea? And what kind of dream does a chickpea have?"

"I want to be more than just food," the chickpea said. "I want to be something that lasts, something that helps others long after I'm gone."

The farmer laughed. "A chickpea is just a chickpea! You have no idea what you're saying."

But as he turned to leave, a breeze carried the chickpea's words back to him. "Even the smallest seed can hold the greatest possibilities."

The farmer paused. Something about the chickpea's words stayed with him. Maybe, just maybe, his wife was right. Maybe blessings didn't always arrive the way we expected.

And with that thought in his heart, he walked back home, leaving the tiny chickpea to begin the greatest adventure of all.

Chapter Two: A Chickpea with a Purpose

That evening, out in the field, the little chickpea felt the cool night air settle over him. He gazed at the sky, where a thousand stars twinkled like scattered pearls.

"There must be more to life than just being eaten," he whispered to himself.

But doubt crept in. What if the farmer was right? What if a chickpea was just a chickpea?

Then, as if the universe had been listening, a gentle gust of wind swirled around him, carrying a soft whisper.

"Hold on to your dream, little one. Your journey has only begun."

And so, as the world slept, the chickpea held onto hope, never knowing that the very next day, his adventure would truly begin.

Meanwhile, as the farmer sat down for dinner, his thoughts kept drifting back to the little chickpea. While putting a bowl of stew in front of him, his wife noticed his silence. She placed a gentle hand on his arm and asked, "Something on your mind?"

The farmer sighed, "You'll think I'm imagining things or losing my mind. I don't quite know what to make of what happened today. I came across a chickpea while I was in the field. And it spoke to me."

His wife smiled, not the least bit surprised. "And what did it say?"

"That it has a dream—to become something greater," the farmer muttered, shaking his head. "And the strangest part? I… I accepted it as my son. It was a mystical experience."

His wife's smile widened. "Then it seems we have received a most unexpected blessing; maybe it wasn't just a chickpea—but one with a purpose."

The farmer let out a deep breath. "I always imagined my son helping me with the farm, ploughing the fields, moving crops, maybe driving a tractor when I grow older. Someone who could carry on for me. Leave a legacy. But… well… he's just a chickpea."

Suddenly, a voice interrupted their conversation. It was the chickpea.

The chickpea chuckled, "I have been here all along, listening to your conversation. And I must say that's where you're wrong, Father. I can help!"

The farmer raised an eyebrow. "Oh really? And how exactly does a chickpea plough a field?"

"Because I have an AI in my head," the chickpea said proudly. "I can drive a tractor, a drone, or even a small helicopter!"

"I also have a good father now who taught me to have a good heart and appreciate my God-given soul. Haven't you been giving me the water of life and nourishing me with love? Don't look at my size—

I am capable. I can help. I can do many things... like use a drone to lift up heavy objects and move them around."

The farmer nearly dropped his spoon. "You… what?!"

"And I know someone—an inventor who lives just behind your garage, who builds machines—drones, tools, and even flying devices that I can use to help you!"

The farmer scratched his head. "You mean the guy next door with thick glasses and long hair?"

"Yes! HE is always nice and clean; besides, we should never judge people by their appearances."

"And how do you plan to pay this genius for making you a drone?"

The chickpea continued, "We can pay him by bartering his services with diamonds!"

Then the chickpea's voice dropped to a whisper. "I know where to find diamonds."

The farmer leaned in closer. "Diamonds?"

"Yes," the chickpea said. "While growing in the soil, I learned the path by observing the water flows from the top of the mountain and by thinking to follow the diamond particles that stopped at the root of my shrub! If we trace it back early in the morning, we'll find the source—and that's where the diamonds are hidden."

The farmer's eyes widened. "You're telling me that a tiny chickpea has figured out where to find diamonds, knows an inventor behind my garage, and can operate a drone?"

The chickpea grinned. "Not just a drone—this one will not only have a magnetic disc to lift objects, but also a special lens to shrink or enlarge them, and it can even let me talk to people and children using a megaphone!"

The farmer leaned back, shaking his head in wonder. "Well… this is certainly not the kind of son I expected. But perhaps… you're exactly the kind of son I needed."

The chickpea wiggled happily. "Father, this is just the beginning. As we go along, I will introduce you to eight more characters—each of them special, each of them with a purpose. But let's take it step by step. First, we need to find the diamonds and meet the inventor."

The farmer smiled, shaking his head. "Step by step, indeed."

And so, with adventure sparkling in their eyes, the farmer and the chickpea prepared for a journey like no other—a journey to uncover the hidden diamonds, meet the brilliant inventor, and build the tools they needed to transform the world.

Little did they know, this was only the beginning.

Chapter Three (Part 1): The Inventor Behind the Garage

Early the next morning, before the sun had fully risen, the farmer and the tiny chickpea made their way to the back of the garage. The air was cool, and the sound of birds waking filled the quiet space. The farmer hesitated.

"Are you sure about this?" he asked.

"Trust me, Father," the chickpea said. "He's a genius."

The farmer knocked on the old wooden door. A few moments later, it creaked open, revealing a thin man with wild hair, thick goggles resting on his forehead, and oil stains all over his clothes. He blinked at them.

"What do you want?" he asked, rubbing his eyes.

The farmer scratched his head. "Well… my son here—" He glanced down at the chickpea, "—has an idea."

The inventor frowned. "Your… son?"

"Yes," the chickpea piped up. "I need a drone—a special one that can lift objects with a powerful magnet, magnify and shrink things, and communicate with large groups of people!"

The inventor stared for a long moment, then took off his goggles and rubbed his face. "I must be dreaming."

"You're not," the chickpea assured him. "I have an AI in my head. I know exactly what we need to build."

The inventor exhaled, crossing his arms. "Well, kid—er, chickpea—it's possible, but it requires a lot of resources: precision parts, advanced materials, and of course, payment to the genius."

The chickpea grinned. "That's where I have a plan. We know where to find diamonds."

The inventor's eyes widened slightly as he asked, "Diamonds?"

The farmer nodded. "The stream from the mountains carries the particles of diamonds down. If we follow it back to its source, we should find them."

The inventor stroked his chin, thinking. "If you can bring me the diamonds, I can build your drone. But this won't be easy. The mountains can be dangerous. And even if you find the diamonds, you'll need to figure out how to carry them back."

The chickpea was unfazed. "We'll find a way."

The inventor studied him carefully, then smiled slightly. "All right, little one. You bring me what I need, and I'll build you the most advanced drone this farm has ever seen."

The chickpea wiggled excitedly. "Then let's get to work!"

And with that, the adventure truly began.

Chapter Three (Part 2): The Harsh Journey—Facing Trials on Dry Land

The sun had barely risen when the farmer strapped on his old leather boots and slung a small sack over his shoulder. The chickpea sat comfortably in the front pocket of his worn-out coat, peeking out with excitement.

"Ready, Father?" the chickpea asked.

The farmer sighed, gazing at the endless stretch of dry land before them. The cracked earth looked unforgiving, and the mountains in the distance seemed impossibly far away.

"As ready as I'll ever be, little one. But I warn you—this land isn't easy to cross."

The chickpea chuckled, "That's why we're not crossing it alone!"

The farmer raised an eyebrow. "What do you mean?"

"I told you before," the chickpea said, "There are others—friends who will join us when the time is right. And I think the first one is just up ahead."

The farmer squinted against the harsh light. In the distance, a whirlwind of dust spun across the land, moving fast. As it came closer, suddenly a bright blue butterfly emerged, its wings shimmering in the sunlight.

"Meet Borboleta," the chickpea announced.

The Creation of the Borboleta Character, the Blue Butterfly

The Amazon Rainforest, vast and teeming with life, is often called the lungs of the planet, breathing in carbon and exhaling the very air that sustains the world. It was there, in the heart of its endless green canopy, that Borboleta, the Blue Butterfly, first took flight. She was born of the wind, dancing among the emerald leaves, her wings shimmering with the hues of the deep sky and rushing rivers.

Borboleta knew every secret of the land—the way the roots whispered to one another beneath the soil, the rhythm of the rain that kissed the treetops, the silent wisdom carried by the oldest trees. She had seen the hands of men carve paths through the forest, some to protect and some to destroy. She had heard the songs of the birds and the sighs of the earth itself. But more than anything, she had felt the subtle power of change—the kind that comes not through force, but slowly rippling outward like waves on the surface of a still pond.

She had often heard humans speak of the Butterfly Effect, the idea that the faintest movement of a butterfly's wings in one corner of the world could set off a cascade of events, shifting the course of history. She believed in this deeply, not just as a scientific concept, but as a spiritual truth.

Borboleta was drawn to roses, lingering where their petals opened in full bloom, savouring their nectar as if tasting the sweetness of creation itself. She listened to the melodies of the Dove of Heaven, the gentle coos of nightingales and canaries, and in their voices, she heard a message: "There is beauty in transformation. There is hope in renewal."

She was not merely a butterfly—she was a guide, a guardian of those whose spirits had curled into cocoons of despair. She hovered near those who had lost all hope, those who had withdrawn from the world, retreating into silence, waiting for something to change.

She understood their pain. She had once been a caterpillar herself, bound to the earth, unaware of what lay ahead. But she had learned that transformation is the result of prolonged reflection—that only through deep contemplation could one truly connect to the spiritual world and emerge renewed.

And so, she whispered encouragement to those in hiding, fluttering close to their hearts.

"Do not fear the darkness of your cocoon," she would say, "For within it, you are not lost—you are becoming."

Borboleta knew that not all who listened would understand, not at first. Some would remain wrapped in their own sorrow, resisting the change they were meant to embrace. But she was patient, for she knew the truth: a single moment of reflection, a single opening of the heart, could eventually come to transform the entire world.

And so, she flew—from the Amazon to the hearts of those who sought light, from one soul to another, leaving behind the softest ripple of change, the faintest movement of hope.

She was the butterfly of awakening, the bearer of a quiet revolution.

And wherever she lingered, transformation would soon follow.

The butterfly fluttered gracefully before landing gently on the farmer's shoulder.

"You must be the wise little seed my friend has spoken of," Borboleta's voice echoed in the gentle breeze.

The farmer blinked, "A talking butterfly. Of course. Why am I even surprised anymore?"

Borboleta chuckled, "You will get used to wonders soon enough. But now, we must move quickly. The desert is not kind to travellers, and the first challenge awaits."

Just then, the wind picked up, and a wall of sand rose before them.

The farmer shielded his eyes and exclaimed, "A sandstorm!"

The chickpea called out, "Borboleta, can you guide us through?"

Borboleta nodded, "Follow my path, and no harm will come to you."

With the butterfly leading the way, they moved forward, step by step, through the raging storm. The farmer gritted his teeth, pushing against the powerful winds, while the chickpea whispered words of encouragement.

"Almost there!" Borboleta called.

After what felt like hours, the storm finally cleared, and they found themselves at the edge of a deep canyon.

The farmer wiped sweat from his brow, "That was... much more than I'd imagined."

The chickpea grinned, "And we've only just begun!"

Borboleta turned toward them, "Ahead lies an even greater test. But don't worry—up ahead, another friend and ally is waiting to help."

The farmer took a deep breath. They had survived their first trial, but the journey had only just begun.

Talking Points for Parents and Their Children:

1. **Overcoming obstacles**– the harsh, dry land and a dangerous sandstorm.

2. **The first companion** – Borboleta, the wise blue butterfly, who guides them through

3. **Foreshadowing** of more trials and characters to come....-the importance of friends along the way

Here's the next section of Chapter Three, introducing **the symbolism of the upcoming characters – and why they are important (Character Symbols Key):** the Australian Shepherd, the Crystal Glass Man, and the Phoenix of Love, while reinforcing their distinct roles in the story.

The Harsh Journey—Facing Trials on Dry Land (Part 2)

The sandstorm had passed, but the dry land ahead still held many dangers. The farmer wiped the sweat from his brow as he looked out over the cracked earth and the canyon stretching before them.

"This journey is tougher than I expected," he admitted.

The chickpea, sitting safely in his coat pocket, grinned. "That's why we're not alone, Father. It's time to meet the next members of our team."

Just then, a sharp bark echoed through the canyon.

The farmer turned just in time to see a strong, swift Australian Shepherd racing towards them, its golden and white fur shimmering under the sun. The dog skidded to a stop, sniffing the air with an alert expression.

"This is the Australian Shepherd," the chickpea said. "He has an incredible nose and senses danger before it happens."

The dog's ears perked up. "And I already smell something unusual ahead," he said. "There's movement in the rocks—something is watching us."

The farmer tensed. "What kind of danger?"

The Australian Shepherd sniffed the wind again. "I don't know yet, but I can track it. If we're careful, we'll get through safely."

The farmer nodded. "Then lead the way."

The dog took the front position, carefully guiding them along the safest path. But just as they reached the next ridge, a dazzling light burst forth from the rocks.

The farmer shielded his eyes. "What now?"

As the light faded, a figure of pure crystal glass stepped out and then stood before them—tall, wise, and shimmering with every colour of the rainbow.

"This," the chickpea whispered in awe, "is the Crystal Glass Man."

The crystal figure bowed slightly. "You have come far, but your journey is not without meaning. Every step you take is part of a greater lesson. What you seek is more than just diamonds—it is transformation."

The farmer swallowed hard. "And what lesson do we learn now?"

The Crystal Glass Man gestured to the canyon below. "Trust—the path ahead requires trust in yourself, trust in your team, and trust in the unseen."

The farmer peered down. A narrow bridge stretched across the canyon, but the ropes looked worn.

"That bridge doesn't look safe," he muttered.

The Crystal Glass Man nodded. "Only with faith can you cross the bridge. And for that, you must listen to the one who understands sacrifice best."

Before the farmer could ask what he meant, a warm wind swirled around them, and a radiant figure appeared in the sky—her wings glowing like fire, her presence both powerful and comforting.

"This is *The Phoenix of Love*," the chickpea whispered, "guardian of resilience and sacrifice."

The Phoenix gazed down at them, her voice filled with warmth. "Every great journey requires courage. Every dream requires sacrifice. If you truly wish to reach the mountains, you must not hesitate. Take the first step, and the rest will follow."

The farmer took a deep breath.

"You mean we have to cross this bridge... without knowing if it will hold?"

The Phoenix of Love nodded. "That is the nature of faith, my friend."

The Australian Shepherd stood beside the farmer. "If we work together, I can sense if something is unstable. Trust my instincts. I will protect you and warn you of unseen dangers," promised the dog.

The Crystal Glass Man extended a hand. "And I will reflect the light you need to see your way."

The Phoenix of Love's fiery wings spread wide. "And I will be here to lift you should you fall."

The farmer tightened his grip on the rope, looking at the unlikely team around him:

- The tiny chickpea with a dream.
- The swift dog with a nose for danger.

- The crystal figure who reflected wisdom.
- The fiery Phoenix who carried the power of love and resilience.

"All right," he said. "Step by step. Let's do this together."

And so, with trust guiding their feet, they took the first step onto the fragile bridge—towards the mountains, the diamonds, and the future that awaited them.

More talking points for discussion between parents and children:

1. **The Australian Shepherd** – loyal, a protector and tracker, warning of unseen dangers.
2. **The Crystal Glass Man** – the guide who teaches wisdom through reflection. Who does he remind you of?
3. **The Phoenix of Love** – the source of resilience, sacrifice, and faith. How can you prepare to recover when you fall down or feel you've failed?
4. **The first major leap of faith** – crossing the canyon using trust and teamwork. How does faith help us to see possibilities that we couldn't see otherwise?

This section included

1. The bridge-crossing scene – how they solve the problems step by step.
2. Facing another unexpected challenge – maybe a hidden threat, a shifting landscape, or a deceptive mirage.
3. How perception and problem-solving play a key role bringing out the strengths of each character.
4. Getting closer to the diamonds but realising something deeper about transformation – setting up Chapter Four.

The Harsh Journey—Facing Trials on Dry Land (Part 3)

The fragile bridge swayed under the farmer's feet as he took his first step. The ropes creaked, and below them, the canyon stretched endlessly, its rocky walls plunging into shadow.

"Stay focused, Father," the chickpea whispered. "Trust the team."

The Australian Shepherd sniffed the air, ears twitching. "The bridge is old, but it will hold if we stay balanced and work together. Move carefully—one step at a time," he said reassuringly.

The Crystal Glass Man lifted his arms, bending them forward in such a way as to catch the sunlight, then gracefully reflected it forward, illuminating the safest path.

The Phoenix of Love soared overhead, her warmth a steady reassurance. "Courage, my friends. The hardest part of any journey is the moment before the leap."

The farmer swallowed his fear and took another tentative step. Then another. Slowly, carefully, the team made their way across.

Just as they reached the halfway point, a deep rumble echoed through the canyon.

"What was that?" the farmer asked, gripping the ropes tighter.

The Australian Shepherd growled. "Something is moving below us."

The Crystal Glass Man's voice was calm: "Not all dangers can be seen at first. Some are hidden beneath the surface."

Suddenly, the bridge jolted violently, shaking beneath their feet.

"Run!" the Phoenix of Love cried.

The farmer broke into a sprint, tightly gripping the ropes as the entire bridge swayed. The Australian Shepherd dashed ahead, leading the way. The chickpea bounced in the farmer's pocket, holding on for dear life.

With a final leap of faith, they made it to the other side just as the bridge collapsed into the canyon below.

The farmer bent over, catching his breath. "That was too close."

The chickpea grinned, exclaiming, "But we made it!"

The Crystal Glass Man nodded. "And now the true test begins," he uttered in a low, sagely voice.

The First Sign of the Diamonds

They walked further into the dry lands, following the winding riverbed that led towards the mountains.

"If my calculations are correct," the chickpea said, "the diamonds should be near the source of this stream. The water carries tiny fragments down to the land below."

The Australian Shepherd sniffed the ground. "There's something strange here. The earth is different."

The farmer knelt, running his fingers through the soil. It sparkled faintly in the sunlight.

"This is it," the farmer whispered.

The Crystal Glass Man touched the ground, his transparent fingers glowing. "Yes, but the diamonds are hidden deep within. You will need more than just strength to reach them."

The Phoenix of Love landed gently beside them. "Before you claim something of great value, you must understand the sacrifice it takes to earn it."

The farmer furrowed his brow. "What do you mean?"

The Phoenix gazed at the land before them. The entrance to the mine was sealed shut, buried under layers of stone.

The Australian Shepherd stepped forward. "I can track the weak points in the rock, the places where we can dig."

The Crystal Glass Man nodded. "And I will reflect the light to show the hidden paths beneath."

The farmer rolled up his sleeves. "Then let's work together and bring these diamonds to the surface."

The True Test of Transformation

They worked tirelessly, chipping away at the hardened soil, following the natural cracks in the rock. The farmer's hands ached, but he pushed on, guided by the insights of his companions.

As they uncovered the first glimmering stone, the Phoenix of Love spoke:

"The diamonds were not simply waiting for you. They had to be earned. Just as you dug through the earth, you must also dig deep within yourself. Every trial you have faced so far—every hardship, every leap of faith—has shaped you into something stronger."

The farmer looked at the gleaming diamond in his hand and understood.

"So… it's not just about finding treasure. It's about becoming worthy of it."

The chickpea beamed. "Exactly, Father! And that's the secret to transformation!"

The Phoenix of Love nodded. "Which is why your next challenge lies ahead."

The farmer looked up towards the towering mountain, where their journey was far from over.

But this time, he wasn't afraid. He had a team. And he was ready.

Transition: The Journey Back from the Mountain

The three pink diamonds sat glistening in the farmer's hands, glowing with a perfect clarity that seemed almost otherworldly. The Australian Shepherd sniffed them curiously, his ears twitching.

"We have what we came for," the farmer said, wiping sweat from his brow, "but now we must get them back to the farm."

The Crystal Glass Man ran his fingers over the diamonds. "These are pure—flawless. But remember, their value is also their weakness. They are delicate. If dropped, they could break."

The Phoenix of Love hovered above them, her fiery wings flickering. "And let's not forget—the bridge we crossed is gone. We need a new way down."

The chickpea wiggled excitedly. "This is where we get creative!"

The Australian Shepherd barked. "I can sniff out a safer route. There's always another path—if you know how to find it."

The team gathered around as the Shepherd led them down a different route—one that was winding, narrow, and hidden beneath the trees, a path few travellers had taken before.

But as they walked, the terrain became steeper, and soon, they found themselves standing at the edge of a deep ravine.

"Another canyon?" the farmer groaned.

"Not just any canyon," the Crystal Glass Man said, his translucent fingers gesturing towards it. "This one is deeper than the last. And there is no bridge."

The Phoenix of Love smiled. "Then we must create our own way across."

The chickpea grinned. "I have an idea. We're holding diamonds, right?"

The farmer raised an eyebrow. "Yes…?"

The chickpea continued excitedly, "Diamonds are strong. They can cut through anything. What if we shape the rocks and form stepping stones across the canyon?"

The Crystal Glass Man's surface gleamed. "Brilliant. But it must be done carefully."

Using a combination of sunlight reflection and careful precision—using the diamonds as a tool—the Crystal Glass Man helped shape the rock edges, forming flat surfaces strong enough to step across.

The farmer tested the first stepping stone. It held.

One by one, step by step, they carefully crossed the canyon until they reached the other side—without losing a single diamond.

The Phoenix of Love hovered above them. "This was your final trial before returning home. You did not simply take the diamonds—you used them wisely."

The Australian Shepherd wagged his tail. "And we did it without breaking a single one!"

The farmer looked down at the glowing diamonds in his hands. "We started this journey thinking these were just treasures. But now I see—they are more than that. They represent everything we've learned along the way."

The chickpea nodded. "And now, we take them back to fulfil our purpose."

With renewed strength, the team descended the final hill and made their way back to the farm—where the genius inventor was awaiting them.

As the chickpea gathered everyone at the farm, he prepared to introduce the Crystal Glass Man and the Phoenix of Love to the genius inventor who was building the helicopter-like drone. But before they could move forward, the chickpea knew it was important to share their deeper story—their origin.

The chickpea took a deep breath and spoke:

"Before we begin, I want you to understand something important. The Crystal Glass Man is not just a wise figure standing before you—he was born from something much deeper, something connected to my father's past."

The farmer listened carefully, sensing the weight in the chickpea's words.

"Many years ago," the chickpea continued, "when my spiritual father lost someone very dear to him, he found himself standing before a glassblower—watching how the craftsman shaped molten glass with fire and breath. He saw how the intense heat, the delicate shaping, and the patience of the glassblower turned something raw and shapeless into something beautiful, both fragile and strong."

The Crystal Glass Man reappeared and nodded, his translucent form catching the morning sunlight.

The Story of the Crystal Glass Man

The chickpea takes a deep breath and says:

"Before we move forward with our plans, I want you to understand something important. The Crystal Glass Man is not just any figure of wisdom. He was born out of something much deeper—something that has to do with my spiritual father's past."

It was a quiet afternoon at the farm, golden fields swaying under the soft breeze. Nokhodee, the little chickpea, sat on the wooden fence beside his father, the farmer. The scent of fresh earth filled the air as the sun cast long shadows over the land.

Nokhodee gazed at the sky, his tiny voice carrying the weight of a memory far older than his little frame.

"Father," he whispered, "have you ever felt like someone you loved never truly left?"

The farmer, wiping the sweat from his brow, looked at his son with quiet curiosity.

"Many times, my son. Those who leave us… they live in our hearts, in the things they taught us, in the way we carry on their work."

Nokhodee nodded, his round little body shifting slightly as he recalled a vision—one that belonged to him yet felt far beyond his own time. He took a deep breath, as if reaching into the depths of his own soul, and spoke:

"I remember a man—a man made of crystal and light. He wasn't born like you and me. He was shaped, formed, through breath and fire. His maker was a master, an artist, who blew his spirit into the molten form, shaping him carefully, giving him life. Each breath of the master moulded him, gave him strength, made him whole.

But then, one day, the master gave his last breath. With a final twist of his cane, he separated the glass figure from its source. And as the master fell, never to rise again, the Crystal Glass Man came to life, beginning to move, taking his first step into this world. He looked at his maker, his spiritual father, and in that moment, he understood. He was born of sacrifice. He was meant to carry on the work of wisdom and service."

Nokhodee fell silent, the warmth of the story settling between them. His father's hands, rough from years of working the land, trembled slightly as he placed them on his lap.

"Where did you hear such a tale, my son?" the farmer asked softly.

Nokhodee turned to him, his small voice filled with certainty.

"I don't know, Father. But it's part of me. As if I carry his spirit inside me as my spiritual father."

The farmer watched his son, a mere chickpea by form, yet something far greater in essence. He reached out and gently touched the tiny seed's side, as if sensing the unseen connection that bound them to something beyond time, beyond the earth they tilled.

"I believe you," he said. "And perhaps, my son, you were meant to carry on a great work as well."

Nokhodee smiled, looking at the vast fields stretching beyond the horizon. He knew, in that moment, that he, too, was shaped by love, strengthened by wisdom, and destined to serve.

And as the breeze whispered through the fields, it carried with it a silent promise—the same promise the Crystal Glass Man had made on the day of his creation:

To carry forth the light of those who came before.

The farmer continued to listen carefully, sensing the weight in the chickpea's words.

"Many years ago," the chickpea continued, "when my spiritual father lost someone very dear to him, he stood before a glassblower—watching how the craftsman shaped the molten glass with his breath and his hands. The intense fire, the delicate shaping, the patience it took to create something both fragile and strong. My father saw in that moment a reflection of life itself: how we are shaped by our trials, refined by fire, and given form by the love and sacrifice of those who came before us."

The Crystal Glass Man reappeared and nodded, his translucent body catching the morning light.

"From that moment on, the spirit of wisdom and sacrifice took shape," the chickpea explained. "And that is how the Crystal Glass Man came into being—formed by the lessons of the past, by the patience of transformation, and by the understanding that nothing truly valuable comes without effort."

The farmer looked at the Crystal Glass Man with new eyes, seeing not just a shimmering figure, but a representation of generations of sacrifice, resilience, and wisdom.

The Legend of the Phoenix of Love

As the fire crackled and sent sparks into the night sky, the Crystal Glass Man's translucent form shimmered, reflecting the dancing flames. The Chickpea, the farmer, and the others gathered closer, drawn by the weight of his words as the Crystal Glass Man spoke:

"You have heard of fire that destroys," he began, his voice carrying the depth of ages. "But have you heard of fire that gives life? This is the story of the Phoenix of Love, the guardian of renewal."

The Chickpea's small heart pounded with anticipation as the Crystal Glass Man continued.

"There once was a time when the world was dark with sorrow. Hearts were heavy, and hope had nearly vanished. But in the midst of despair, there existed one soul so radiant, so filled with love, that even the darkness could not consume her.

"She was a woman of many forms—a mother who nurtured, a daughter who carried dreams, a sister who stood against oppression, a wife who loved unconditionally, a teacher who awakened minds. She gave endlessly—her wisdom, her strength, her very life—so that others might rise. And when the world turned against her, when her love was met with rejection, when her sacrifices were dismissed, she did not crumble. No. She burned with a fire so bright that even the heavens took notice."

The Phoenix of Love stood tall and proud, the fire of love emanating from her wings, then crackling louder as the Crystal Glass Man continued his tale.

"And then," the Crystal Glass Man continued, his voice softer now, "she suddenly disappeared, later to return."

The Crystal Glass Man continued, his voice softer now. "The world, for a moment, felt empty. But love does not die. Love always stays with us and transforms those who experience it.

"However, before she disappeared, she stood before those who sought to silence the roaring of her fiery wings. She did not tremble. Instead, she spoke the words that would echo across time:

'You can take my life, but you can never stop the emancipation of women.'

"And with those words, she became immortal.

"They took her life. But from the ashes of her sacrifice, a single spark remained. A breeze, gentle yet powerful, carried that ember across the lands, across generations. It found its way into the hearts of those who still believed in love, those who still sacrificed, those who still nurtured others despite pain and loss. And from that ember, the Phoenix of Love was born."

The Chickpea's breath caught in his throat. He turned to the Phoenix of Love, who had now reappeared, standing beside them, her wings glowing softly, like the embers of a heart that would never stop burning.

"She rises when a mother cradles her child with devotion," the Crystal Glass Man continued. "She rises when a sister stands against injustice. She rises when a wife gives her heart to heal another. She rises when a teacher imparts knowledge to awaken minds. She rises when a daughter carries forward a dream for future generations.

And she will always rise.

She is the fire that tempers the steel of our souls. She is the warmth that melts cruelty into compassion. She is the light that turns loss into renewal."

The Chickpea swallowed hard again, understanding now that the Phoenix of Love was more than just a legend—she was alive in the sacrifices of all those who came before him.

"You are the fire that gives life," the Chickpea whispered.

The Phoenix of Love knelt before the Crystal Glass Man, her golden eyes filled with infinite wisdom.

"And so are you," she said gently. "One day, you too will understand the power of sacrifice, and when that time comes, you will rise anew."

The wind stirred, carrying the last echoes of the legend into the night, as the stars above shone just a little brighter.

The Phoenix of Love spread her fiery wings, her voice calm yet filled with ancient knowledge.

"I am the guardian of renewal," she said. "Every time a person loves deeply and sacrifices for the good of others, a part of me is reborn. Your father, dear farmer, showed love and sacrifice in ways few understood. That is why I have come—to remind you that from loss, new beginnings always rise."

"In that moment," the Chickpea explained, "my father realized that life itself is like glass—we are shaped by our trials, refined by fire, and given form by the love and sacrifices of those who came before us. And so, the spirit of wisdom and endurance took shape, and that is how the Crystal Glass Man came into being."

Now the farmer looked at the Crystal Glass Man again, but this time with new eyes, seeing not just a shimmering figure, but a reflection of generations of sacrifice, resilience, and wisdom.

Then, the Chickpea turned to the Phoenix of Love, his voice filled with admiration, and said:

"And then, there is the Phoenix of Love. She, too, was born from sacrifice. Each time she faces destruction, she rises again, stronger, more radiant, carrying the lessons of every past generation within her wings."

The Phoenix of Love spread her fiery wings, her voice calm yet powerful.

"I am the guardian of renewal," she said. "Every time a person loves deeply and sacrifices for the good of others, a part of me is reborn. Your father, dear farmer, showed love and sacrifice in ways few understood. That is why I have come—to remind you that from loss, always a new beginning arises."

The farmer stood in silence, absorbing these words.

For the first time, he truly understood: transformation is not just about change—it is about recognizing the love, wisdom, and sacrifices of those who came before us.

And with that, the journey towards something far greater had begun.

Chapter Four: The Five Stages of Transformation

The early morning mist settled over the farm as the chickpea and the farmer stood before the Crystal Glass Man and the Phoenix of Love. The drone, now halfway built, sat in the inventor's workshop, its sleek frame glinting under the rising sun.

The Crystal Glass Man said, "As some of you already know, the chickpea may only qualify to transition from the dryland into the ocean after he goes through five stages of transformation."

The chickpea turned to the Phoenix of Love: "You said transformation comes in stages. But what exactly does that mean?"

The Phoenix of Love spread her radiant wings, her voice warm and full of wisdom: "True transformation does not happen all at once. It unfolds in five stages—each one shaping you into something greater. These five stages of transformation that we are going to talk about are stages of society that have shaped civilizations and shaped their heroes like Galileo and Einstein."

The farmer crossed his arms, intrigued. "Then tell us. What are these five stages?"

The Phoenix nodded and began.

Stage One: The Awakening

"Every great transformation begins with an awakening," the Phoenix said. "It is the moment you realize that the world is bigger than what you once believed and that you are meant for something more."

The chickpea nodded. "That moment was when I first whispered my dream in the field—when I knew I was more than just another chickpea waiting to be eaten."

The farmer exhaled slowly. "For me, it was when you spoke to me for the first time. That moment you shared your vision—it changed everything."

The Crystal Glass Man stepped forward. "Awakening is the first step, but it is not enough. Many awaken, but few take the next step."

Stage Two: The Trial

"Once you awaken," the Phoenix continued, "you must face trials. These challenges test your resolve. They push you to your limits. This is where many fall back into their old ways."

The farmer nodded. "Like when we crossed the canyon. If we had turned back, we would never have found the diamonds."

The Australian Shepherd barked, "And the sandstorm—that was a trial too. We had to trust Borboleta to guide us."

The Phoenix of Love smiled. "Exactly. Trials are meant to refine you, just as fire refines gold. But passing a trial does not mean transformation is complete. There is still more."

Stage Three: The Sacrifice

The Crystal Glass Man's surface shimmered. "To transform, one must give up something. A comfort. A fear. A false belief. True change always requires sacrifice."

The farmer was silent for a moment. "I had to let go of what I thought a son should be. I had to embrace the unexpected."

The chickpea smiled. "And I had to leave my safe home in the field to become something greater."

The Phoenix of Love spoke softly. "Many turn back at this stage because sacrifice is painful. But only those who embrace it can reach the next stage."

Stage Four: The Rebirth

"Once you have sacrificed, you are no longer the same," the Phoenix said. "You begin to see with new eyes. This is the stage where you are reborn—not as who you were, but as who you are meant to be."

The chickpea thought for a moment. "That's what happened to the diamonds. They were hidden, buried beneath the earth. They had to be uncovered and shaped before they could shine."

The Crystal Glass Man nodded. "And just like glass is melted and reshaped, transformation remakes us into something new."

The farmer looked at his hands, calloused from work. "I have been a farmer my whole life. But maybe now, I am becoming something more."

The Phoenix of Love's wings glowed brighter. "And that leads to the final stage."

Stage Five: The Legacy

"True transformation does not end with you," the Phoenix said. "Once you have awakened, endured trials, made sacrifices, and been reborn—you must share what you have learned. You must leave something behind that others can follow."

The farmer's eyes widened. "That's why we are building the drone. Not just for us, but to serve others."

The chickpea looked around at the team. "And that's why I was never meant to do this alone. My legacy is not just about me—it's about what we build together."

The Phoenix of Love smiled. "Now you understand."

The Crystal Glass Man placed a hand on the drone. "And this will be the first of many tools to help shape the future."

The farmer took a deep breath. "Then it's time to finish what we started."

The chickpea grinned. "Yes. And after that, there are still more friends to meet."

And with that, they turned toward the future—ready for the next step in their journey.

More Points for discussion:

1. The Five Stages of Transformation – A structured way to show how true change happens.

2. How Each Stage Relates to the Characters – Making the lessons personal and meaningful.

3. The characters and how they connect to Their Mission – Their transformation is leading to something greater.

4. Builds Anticipation – The drone is almost ready, but more adventures lie ahead!

Back at the Farm: The Genius Prepares the Drone

By the time they reached the farm, the sun was just beginning to set. The air smelled of warm earth, and the familiar sight of the old garage was a welcome relief.

The genius inventor was waiting at the door, arms crossed, goggles perched on his head.

"You actually did it?" he said, his eyes widening as the farmer held up the three flawless pink diamonds.

"We did," the chickpea said proudly. "And we carried them back safely, just as you warned us."

The inventor whistled. "Well, well. Then it's time for me to do my part. These diamonds are exactly what I need to finish the drone."

He took the diamonds carefully, placing them on his workbench.

"It will take a little time," he said, rubbing his hands together, "but I'll craft something better than you ever imagined."

The chickpea beamed. "While we wait, I want you to meet two very important friends."

He gestured towards the Crystal Glass Man and the Phoenix of Love.

"They both have stories that go beyond this farm—beyond even this world. Their wisdom is shaped by generations of sacrifice. And before this journey is over, we will need to understand their lessons fully."

The farmer nodded. "Then let's hear their stories."

As the sun dipped below the horizon, the team gathered under the old tree, ready to listen, to learn, and to prepare for the next phase of their adventure.

Because their mission was only just beginning.

More Talking point

The problem of carrying the diamonds safely was solved—they find an alternative route and use the diamonds to create stepping stones across a canyon. Think of what were the important factors that helped:

1. They don't just take the diamonds; they use them wisely, showing that their journey has taught them something deeper, which demonstrates growth.

2. They return safely to the farm, deliver the diamonds, and set the stage for the genius inventor to finish the drone—a smooth transition to the next step.

3. Before moving forward, the team takes a moment to reflect on their wisdom. - What have the Phoenix of Love and Crystal Glass Man taught?

Chapter Five: The Call of the Ocean

The morning air was crisp as the genius inventor stepped out of his workshop, wiping grease from his hands. His eyes gleamed with satisfaction as he looked at the team gathered before him.

"Well, my friends, it's done," he said.

The farmer, the chickpea, and the rest of the team leaned in as he uncovered the drone—a sleek, powerful machine shaped like a miniature helicopter, its blades gleaming in the sunlight.

The chickpea gasped, "It's perfect!"

The Crystal Glass Man examined it carefully, his transparent fingers tracing its smooth surface. "It is not just a machine. It is a tool for transformation," he said.

The Phoenix of Love nodded, "But where it takes you next will determine your destiny."

The farmer furrowed his brow. "Where it takes us? You mean we aren't done yet?"

The chickpea wiggled with excitement. "Of course not, Father! This was just the beginning! There's another part of the journey waiting for us—the ocean."

The farmer blinked. "The ocean? But why?"

The Crystal Glass Man's surface shimmered, reflecting the sky. "Because what you seek is not just on land. The greatest transformations often come from the depths of the unknown."

The Phoenix of Love spread her wings. "And there is something waiting for you there. Something that will complete the next stage of your journey."

The genius inventor adjusted his goggles. "Your drone is ready. It can carry objects, magnify or shrink them, and communicate with people over long distances. But to reach the ocean safely, you'll need to test it first."

The chickpea nodded. "Then let's fly!"

Testing the Drone and the Journey to the Ocean

The Australian Shepherd wagged his tail. "Before we go anywhere, I should scout ahead. There may be dangers on the road."

The drone lifted off for the first time, hovering gracefully in the air, its magnifying lens glowing as it scanned the landscape.

The farmer watched in awe. "It's incredible."

The Crystal Glass Man nodded. "But a tool is only as good as those who wield it. You must learn to use it wisely."

The Phoenix of Love gazed towards the horizon. "The ocean is far, and the journey will not be easy. But within its waters lies the next key to transformation."

The farmer sighed, looking at the chickpea. "Are you sure about this, little one?"

The chickpea grinned. "Absolutely, Father. The ocean is calling us. And we must answer."

And so, with the drone leading the way, the team set off towards the unknown—towards the ocean, where the next great mystery awaited.

Points for more discussion

1. What led to the completion of the Drone – that is now ready for action.
2. Explain -what the Chickpea needs to do before he is accepted into the Ocean – A new phase of transformation awaits.
3. Let's prepare for the Next Challenge – The journey will not be easy.
4. Builds Anticipation for the Next Character – Who will they meet in the ocean?

A Crucial Point!

Before the chickpea (TSP) can qualify to go deep into the ocean, he must demonstrate his worthiness by serving others—especially children. This means we need to show acts of service, kindness, and problem-solving that prove he is ready for the next stage of transformation.

This will give us a strong foundation before he reaches the ocean, making the journey feel earned, meaningful, and impactful.

Serving Others First, Before Attending the Call of the Ocean

As the drone hovered in the air, the Crystal Glass Man and the Phoenix of Love exchanged knowing glances.

"Before you can go to the ocean," the Crystal Glass Man said, "you must first prove that you are ready."

The chickpea blinked. "But didn't we already prove ourselves on the mountain?"

The Phoenix of Love shook her head. "Overcoming trials for yourself is one thing, but true transformation comes when you serve others."

The farmer frowned. "What must we do?"

The Crystal Glass Man's surface shimmered. "There are children who need your help. If you truly seek wisdom, you must first give freely of what you have."

The chickpea sat up. "Then let's find them!"

Helping the Children: Three Acts of Service

The drone scanned the horizon, its magnifying lens searching for those in need. It didn't take long before it found its first mission.

1. Rescuing the Lost Child

Near the edge of some farmlands, a small child had wandered too far from home and was lost in a thick grove of trees. The Australian Shepherd barked urgently.

"I smell fear. A child is in trouble."

The farmer nodded. "We must find them before nightfall."

Using the drone's camera and heat sensors, they quickly spotted the lost child huddled under a tree. The chickpea spoke through the drone's megaphone in a gentle voice, addressing the child:

"Don't be afraid! We're here to help you!"

The Phoenix of Love soared ahead, lighting the way. The Australian Shepherd led the farmer through the trees, guiding them to the child.

With teamwork and quick thinking, they safely returned the child home.

2. Bringing Water to the Village

As the Chick Pea and his team continued their journey, they came across a small village where children were struggling to carry heavy buckets of water.

"The well is far away," one of them explained. "It takes us all day just to bring enough water for our families."

The Crystal Glass Man studied the landscape. "This land is dry. But there is water beneath the surface."

The Chick Pea turned to the farmer. "Can we use the drone to help?"

The inventor adjusted the drone's settings. "If we modify its magnifying lens, we can create a small irrigation system that pulls water up from the ground."

With careful precision, they redirected an underground water source to flow into the village, giving the children and their families easier access to fresh water.

The children cheered, "Thank you!"

3. Teaching and Inspiring the Next Generation

That evening, as they rested near the edge of the coast, a group of children gathered around the team, curious about the talking Chick Pea and the magical drone.

The Chick Pea smiled, "We all have the power to dream big. No matter where you come from, you can do great things."

The farmer told them stories of courage. The Phoenix of Love spoke of resilience. The Crystal Glass Man taught them about wisdom.

The children listened in awe, their eyes shining with inspiration.

"One day, we want to be like you!" they said.

The Phoenix of Love nodded, "And one day, you will be even greater than us."

The Ocean Beckons

As dawn approached, the team stood by the shore, gazing at the vast blue ocean ahead.

The Phoenix of Love spread her wings, "You have served well. You have given to others without expecting anything in return. Now, the ocean calls you forward."

The Crystal Glass Man placed a hand on the drone, "The greatest lessons often lie in the places we fear the most. Are we ready to face our fears?"

The Chick Pea took a deep breath, "Yes. We're ready. Failures, though often feared and avoided, are rich sources of learning."

And so, with the drone leading the way, they stepped forward— towards the next great adventure.

More thing to talk about:

1. Demonstrates Worthiness – The Chick Pea and his team prove they are ready to go deeper into transformation by serving others.

2. Shows Three Acts of Service —

    - Rescuing a lost child
    - Bringing water to a village
    - Teaching and inspiring children

3. Creates a Strong Transition to the Ocean – Now that they have helped others, they are spiritually ready to enter the next phase of their journey.

Chapter Six: The Leap of Faith—Jumping into the Waters

The golden rays of dawn shimmered over the vast ocean, stretching endlessly before them. The farmer, the chickpea, and their loyal team stood at the water's edge, gazing at the rolling waves.

"It's beautiful," the farmer murmured.

The Phoenix of Love hovered above them, her wings glowing like embers in the morning light. "It is more than beautiful—it is powerful. And it is waiting for you."

The Crystal Glass Man touched the surface of the water. "Beyond these waves lies knowledge that can only be gained by those who are willing to take the leap."

The chickpea wiggled in excitement. "Then let's go!"

The farmer hesitated. "Hold on, little one. How are we supposed to cross? We don't have a boat."

The Australian Shepherd sniffed the salty air, ears perked. "There's something in the water. I can sense it."

The drone hovered over the waves, scanning the depths. Its magnifying lens flickered, revealing a hidden figure beneath the surface.

The chickpea stood at the shore, hesitant about stepping into the ocean's unknown depths.

The Australian Shepherd suddenly stopped, sniffing the air, ears alert. His stance tightened.

"There's something in the water. I can sense it."

The waves looked calm, but the Shepherd's warning was clear—something lurked beneath the surface.

He nudged the chickpea back, positioning himself as a barrier between the unknown and his team.

Then, suddenly—a large, elegant creature emerged.

All the characters, being so impressed by the Australian Shepherd, each commented on his special qualities:

The chickpea, surprisingly, commented, "I don't know how he knows these things, but I trust him. When I am afraid, I look into his eyes and see certainty."

The chickpea saw him as an anchor of safety, a protector whose instincts were always right.

The Crystal Glass Man (CGMan) added, "His senses are sharper than mine. I see the world through reflections, but he sees the unseen. He reminds me to trust what I cannot always perceive."

The Phoenix of Love then admired him by saying, "He is not just a dog. He is love in its purest, most loyal form."

Borboleta (The Blue Butterfly), comparing him with her own strengths, remarked, "His feet stay on the ground, but his heart flies like mine. He knows things we cannot hear, see, or touch."

The Dolphin: The Guide of the Deep

The water parted as a sleek, intelligent dolphin surfaced, its silver-blue skin glistening in the sun. It let out a cheerful clicking sound, observing the team with bright, knowing eyes.

The chickpea gasped, "It's you! I've heard stories about you!"

The dolphin circled gracefully. "And I have been waiting for you."

The farmer raised an eyebrow. "You know us?"

The dolphin nodded. "I know all who seek wisdom. The ocean does not reveal its secrets to just anyone. Only those who serve others, who give more than they take, are invited into its depths."

The Phoenix of Love smiled. "That is why you were tested before coming here."

The dolphin clicked again. "If you are ready, I will take you beyond the waves. But once you go beneath the surface, you must trust the journey—because you will not be the same when you return."

The chickpea grinned, "We are ready!"

The farmer hesitated. "Are you sure about this?"

The Crystal Glass Man stepped forward. "Transformation always requires a leap of faith."

The Phoenix of Love nodded. "And sometimes, the only way forward is to dive into the unknown."

The farmer took a deep breath, looking at the vast ocean before them. Then, slowly, he nodded.

"Alright," he said, "let's do this."

The dolphin let out an excited trill.

"Then hold on tight!"

The Dive into the Unknown

One by one, they stepped into the water, the cool waves rushing around them.

The Australian Shepherd swam beside them, paddling through the gentle currents.

The drone hovered above, scanning and recording everything.

The dolphin led the way, diving beneath the surface.

And then—with a final deep breath—they plunged into the depths of the ocean.

The world around them changed instantly.

The surface disappeared above, replaced by endless blue. Light shimmered in liquid patterns, and strange, beautiful creatures swam past, their colours glowing like stars in the deep.

The chickpea spun in amazement. "This is incredible!"

The farmer's voice was full of awe. "I never imagined a world like this existed beneath the surface."

The dolphin swam beside them, guiding them deeper. "You have stepped into a new reality. Here, the rules of the land do not apply. Here, you will learn a different kind of wisdom."

The Crystal Glass Man's body glowed in the refracted light. "Everything we think we know is only a small part of the truth. The deeper we go, the more we see."

The Phoenix of Love's wings shimmered above the water. "But be prepared. Just as the land had its trials, the ocean will test you too."

The farmer nodded. "We're ready."

And with that, they followed the dolphin deeper, into the mysteries of the ocean.

Their greatest adventure had just begun.

Points for discussion:

1. Introduces the Dolphin – A wise and friendly guide who will lead them into the depths.
2. Marks the Leap of Faith – They must trust the ocean and embrace the unknown.
3. Sets the Stage for New Challenges – The ocean will test them, just as the dry land did.
4. Shifts the Story to a New Realm – Moving from the earthly world to the world beneath the sea.

Chapter Seven: The Koi Fish and the Dolphin—Lessons of Transformation

The chickpea and his team drifted deeper into the ocean, following the dolphin's smooth, graceful movements. The light above grew fainter, replaced by a deep blue glow that pulsed like a heartbeat.

The farmer exhaled slowly, marvelling at the vastness around him.

"It's like stepping into another world."

The Crystal Glass Man's translucent body shimmered with the shifting light.

"Because it *is* another world. One that holds wisdom the land cannot teach."

The dolphin clicked softly.

"But before you can reach the deepest part of the ocean, you must pass another test."

The chickpea tilted his head.

"Another test? But we already proved ourselves on land!"

The Phoenix of Love's wings flickered, even underwater.

"Transformation never ends, little one. With each step forward, a new challenge arises."

The dolphin nodded.

"And this time, your guide will not be me—it will be the Koi Fish."

The Arrival of the Koi Fish

Just then, a golden-orange glow appeared in the water ahead.

A majestic koi fish swam towards them, its long, flowing fins rippling like silk. Its scales shimmered with hues of red, gold, and white.

The farmer whispered in awe,

"I've heard legends of koi fish that transform into dragons. Is it true?"

The Koi Fish circled them gracefully.

"The legends speak of a journey. A koi fish that swims against the current and reaches the highest waterfall is transformed. But not all koi reach their destiny—only those who endure."

The chickpea's eyes widened.

"So, you've been through a transformation too?"

The Koi Fish dipped its head.

"Every being must go through trials. Now, you must pass yours."

The farmer glanced at the dolphin.

"What do we have to do?"

The dolphin flicked its tail.

"You must enter the heart of the ocean, where the great oysters dwell. But only one of you can go inside."

The chickpea's heart raced.

"Inside? You mean… inside an oyster?"

The Crystal Glass Man's voice was calm.

"This is your next transformation, little one. Just as a grain of sand enters an oyster and becomes a pearl, you must enter and let the ocean shape you."

The farmer looked at the tiny chickpea.

"Are you sure about this?"

The chickpea straightened.

"I was born to transform, Father. This is the next step."

The Koi Fish nodded.

"Then follow me."

The Journey to the Oyster –

The team swam deeper into the ocean, following the Koi Fish through tunnels of coral and shimmering schools of fish. The water grew darker, but the Crystal Glass Man reflected what little light remained, guiding them forward.

Finally, they reached a hidden valley at the bottom of the ocean—where giant oysters rested, their shells closed tightly, guarding their secrets.

The dolphin spoke softly.

"One of these oysters will accept you. But you must listen to the ocean and choose wisely."

The chickpea floated before the oysters, feeling a pull towards one in particular.

"This one," he whispered.

The Koi Fish's golden fins shimmered.

"Then enter, and let the ocean shape you."

The farmer swallowed hard.

"I will be right here when you come out, little one."

The chickpea nodded, then took a deep breath.

And with that, he entered the oyster's shell, letting it close around him, surrendering to the mystery of transformation.

Points for discussion:

1. Introduces the Koi Fish – A symbol of perseverance and transformation.

2. Explains the Next Trial – The chickpea must enter an oyster to complete his transformation.

3. Builds Suspense – What will happen inside the oyster? How will the chickpea change?

4. Sets Up the Next Chapter – The chickpea's transformation into the Pearl of Wisdom begins.

Chapter Eight: The Pearl Maker's Secret—Inside the Oyster

The world outside faded as the oyster's shell closed around the chickpea. The ocean's whispers became distant, and for the first time, there was only silence.

The chickpea floated in darkness, unsure of what would come next.

"Is this it?" he thought. "Nothing is happening."

He waited.

And waited.

Time seemed to stretch endlessly. There was no light, no movement—only the quiet pressure of the oyster's embrace.

Then, a deep, ancient voice echoed through the silence.

"You have entered the chamber of patience," the voice said.

The chickpea's tiny heart raced. "Who are you?"

"I am the Pearl Maker," the voice responded, "and I have been waiting for you."

The Secret of the Pearl Maker

A soft glow began to fill the darkness, illuminating the swirling interior of the oyster. The chickpea felt a warm, protective energy wrap around him.

"You wish to transform," the Pearl Maker continued, "but transformation does not happen instantly. Just as a pearl takes time to form, so must you."

The chickpea hesitated. "But I've already learned so much. I crossed the dry lands, found the diamonds, served the children, and took the leap into the ocean. Why must I wait?"

A gentle ripple moved through the oyster's walls.

"Because true wisdom is not rushed. It is layered, one experience at a time—just like a pearl. The more patience you have, the more radiant you will become."

The chickpea fell silent, absorbing these words.

"So… I must wait?"

"Yes. And as you wait, the ocean will shape you."

The Layers of Transformation

Days passed. Or maybe weeks. Or months. Time inside the oyster was different.

The chickpea felt himself changing, layer by layer, as the Pearl Maker coated him in luminous wisdom.

He thought about his journey.

He remembered the farmer's love and Borboleta's guidance.

He recalled the Australian Shepherd's loyalty and the Crystal Glass Man's wisdom.

He held onto the Phoenix of Love's lessons about sacrifice and renewal.

And he thought about the children he had helped.

With every memory, another layer formed around him—stronger, brighter, more complete.

Until finally, the Pearl Maker's voice returned.

"It is done. You are ready."

The oyster shell trembled. Light seeped through the cracks.

And then—with a soft, glowing pulse—the oyster slowly opened.

The Emergence of the Pearl of Wisdom

Outside, the farmer and his companions had waited patiently, watching over the oyster.

The dolphin swam in circles, sensing that the moment had arrived.

The Koi Fish lifted its golden fins, bowing in respect.

The Crystal Glass Man's surface glowed softly.

And the Phoenix of Love spread her wings.

"He is coming."

A gentle light radiated from inside the oyster. The shell creaked open, revealing—

The Pearl of Wisdom.

Where the chickpea once was, now lay a shimmering pearl, glowing with a wisdom deeper than the ocean itself.

The farmer gasped. "Little one… is that you?"

The pearl pulsed gently. Then, slowly, it lifted from the shell and floated towards them, as if carried by an unseen force.

A soft, familiar voice spoke—no longer just a whisper, but a voice full of clarity, strength, and purpose.

"Father, I have returned."

Points for discussion:

1. Completes the Chickpea's Transformation – He becomes the Pearl of Wisdom.

2. Reveals the Secret of the Pearl Maker – Wisdom is formed through patience and experience.

3. Creates a Powerful Moment of Rebirth – The team witnesses the transformation.

4. Prepares for the Next Phase of the Journey – What does the Pearl of Wisdom do next?

Chapter Nine: The Return to the Surface—A New Mission Begins

The Pearl of Wisdom hovered above the open oyster shell, its soft glow illuminating the ocean depths. The team watched in silence—the farmer, the dolphin, the Koi Fish, the Crystal Glass Man, and the Phoenix of Love.

The farmer took a step forward, his voice filled with awe. "You've changed, little one. You are no longer just a chickpea."

The Pearl of Wisdom pulsed gently. "No, Father. I have become something more. And now, it is time to use what I have learned."

The dolphin nodded. "Then you are ready to return to the surface."

The Koi Fish swirled around them, its golden fins shimmering. "But remember—true wisdom is only valuable if it is shared. What will you do with the knowledge you now possess?"

The Pearl of Wisdom paused.

"I will bring this wisdom to the world—a world trapped in economic warfare and survival struggles. The ocean has taught me patience, resilience, and the power of transformation. But now, I must apply it where it is needed most."

The Crystal Glass Man stepped forward, his translucent form reflecting the Pearl's glow.

"The world above is in turmoil. The pursuit of wealth has blinded many, and economic warfare threatens the balance of life itself. If you truly wish to bring wisdom, you must challenge these false illusions."

The Phoenix of Love spread her radiant wings.

"You must teach the world that prosperity is not built on greed, but on service, balance, and justice."

The farmer nodded slowly. "Then let us return. There is much work to do."

The Rise to the Surface

The team swam upward, following the dolphin as they ascended through the shifting blue waters.

With each passing moment, the light grew brighter. They were rising not just toward the surface, but toward a new purpose.

Finally, they broke through the waves, emerging under a sky painted with the golden hues of sunrise.

The farm was visible in the distance, but something had changed. The world no longer looked the same.

The Pearl of Wisdom hovered beside the farmer. "I see now what I could not see before. The struggles of mankind are not only physical but deeply rooted in thought, perception, and structure. We must begin by reshaping the way people understand prosperity."

The Crystal Glass Man's voice was steady. "Then let us begin where transformation always starts—with awareness."

The New Mission: Ending Economic Warfare

As they stepped onto the shore, the Pearl of Wisdom turned to the farmer.

"Father, tell me—what do people fight for the most?"

The farmer exhaled. "Resources. Power. Control. They believe wealth will bring them happiness, but they chase it without understanding its purpose."

The Phoenix of Love's wings flickered. "Then we must teach them a different way."

The Australian Shepherd barked, his tail wagging. "And we must be careful. Those who profit from division will not welcome your wisdom so easily."

The Pearl of Wisdom pulsed with understanding.

"Then we must act wisely. We will not fight against them—we will offer them something greater. A vision of prosperity that is built on unity, not competition. On service, not greed."

The Crystal Glass Man nodded.

"Then let us begin the next phase of our journey—bringing wisdom to a world that does not yet know it needs it."

And so, with the dawn of a new day, the team set forth—not as wanderers, but as guides, carrying a vision that could transform the world itself.

Points for Discussion on what this chapter accomplishes:

1. Returns the Pearl of Wisdom to the surface – Now transformed, he is ready to act.
2. Defines the next challenge – Applying wisdom to economic warfare and global struggles.
3. Sets the stage for action – The team will begin reshaping perspectives on wealth and prosperity.
4. Introduces conflict – Those who profit from economic warfare will resist change.

Chapter Ten: The First Challenge—Breaking the Illusions of Wealth

The Pearl of Wisdom and the team stood at the edge of the farm, looking beyond the familiar fields towards the cities, banks, and towering industries that controlled the world's economy.

The farmer adjusted his hat. "So, where do we begin?"

The Crystal Glass Man's voice was calm. "We begin by breaking the greatest illusion of all—the belief that wealth equals power."

The Phoenix of Love spread her fiery wings. "For too long, people have measured their worth by what they own, not by what they give. The world is trapped in a cycle of economic warfare, greed, and fear."

The Australian Shepherd sniffed the air. "And those who control wealth will not let go of their power easily."

The Pearl of Wisdom pulsed with clarity.

"Then we must show them a new way."

The City of Gold and Shadows

The team travelled beyond the farm, into the heart of a great city—the City of Gold and Shadows.

Towering glass skyscrapers stretched towards the sky, reflecting sunlight like diamonds. But beneath them, in the streets below, poverty thrived.

The rich dined in luxury, while children begged for food.

The farmer clenched his fists. "How can there be so much wealth, yet so much suffering?"

The Crystal Glass Man touched the pavement. "Because the system was built on illusion. Wealth was never meant to be hoarded. It was meant to be shared, circulated, and used for the betterment of all."

The Phoenix of Love gazed at the city. "But those who rule from the towers above will not easily change their ways."

The Pearl of Wisdom turned towards the tallest building—the Tower of Wealth, where the most powerful leaders gathered.

"Then we must go to them."

The Council of the Wealthy

Inside the Tower of Wealth, the most powerful economic leaders in the world sat in a grand chamber, discussing trade, investments, and strategies to keep their control intact.

When the Pearl of Wisdom entered the room, the council fell silent.

A man in a black suit, adorned with gold rings, sneered. "Who dares interrupt us?"

The Pearl of Wisdom's soft glow filled the chamber. "I have come to offer you something greater than wealth—true prosperity."

The council members laughed.

"Prosperity? We already own everything. We have no need for your wisdom."

The Pearl pulsed gently. "Then tell me, if you are so rich, why do you live in fear?"

The room grew still.

The Phoenix of Love stepped forward. "You fear losing what you have built. You fear the poor rising up. You fear each other. That is not wealth—that is imprisonment."

The Crystal Glass Man's voice was steady. "True prosperity does not come from hoarding riches. It comes from creating a system where all can thrive, where no one is left behind."

The man in the black suit smirked. "And why should we care? The system works for us."

The Pearl of Wisdom's glow intensified. "Because the system is collapsing. If you do not change, the world will change without you."

The council members shifted uneasily. They knew the world was on the brink of rebellion. They knew inequality could not last forever.

"And what do you propose?" one finally asked.

The Pearl of Wisdom spoke with certainty.

"A new economy—one based on service, not greed. On balance, not excess. On sustainability, not destruction. The wealth you hoard must be transformed into opportunity for all."

The council members scoffed. "And if we refuse?"

The Phoenix of Love's eyes burned like fire. "Then you will watch as your towers crumble under the weight of your own greed."

The Crystal Glass Man nodded. "Change is coming. You can be part of it or be left behind."

For the first time, the leaders of wealth felt something they had never felt before—not power, but the weight of truth.

They were at a crossroads.

Would they listen, or would they resist?

The battle for the future had begun.

Points for Discussion on what this chapter accomplishes:

1. **Takes the Fight to the Heart of the System** – The team confronts economic rulers directly.
2. **Challenges the Illusions of Wealth** – Money without purpose is not prosperity—it is fear.
3. **Presents a New Vision** – A world where wealth serves humanity, not the other way around.

4. **Sets Up the Conflict** – The leaders of wealth must choose—change or be left behind.

Chapter Eleven: The Resistance—When the Powerful Refuse to Change

The council chamber inside the Tower of Wealth was silent. The Pearl of Wisdom's glow pulsed steadily, waiting for an answer.

The wealthy leaders, draped in fine suits and adorned with gold, exchanged glances. Some looked uncertain. Others sneered.

The man in the black suit leaned forward, his voice sharp.

"You speak of balance, of sharing wealth, of ending greed. But let me ask you—why should we give up what we have built?"

The Crystal Glass Man stepped forward.

"Because what you have built is unsustainable. You see only short-term gain, but the world is collapsing under the weight of inequality."

The Phoenix of Love's wings flickered.

"People are suffering while you hoard resources. You cannot call that success."

A woman with diamond-studded rings scoffed.

"This is the way of the world. There have always been the rich and the poor. That is how civilisation survives."

The Pearl of Wisdom pulsed.

"No. That is how civilisation crumbles."

The council members murmured among themselves.

But the man in the black suit stood up, slamming his hands on the table.

"Enough of this nonsense! We control the banks. We control the markets. Do you really think a glowing pearl and a handful of dreamers can change that?"

The Australian Shepherd growled softly, sensing danger.

The farmer took a deep breath.

"We are not here to threaten you. We are here to offer you a choice."

The Pearl of Wisdom's glow brightened.

"You have two paths before you. One leads to a new world—where wealth serves humanity, not controls it. The other leads to collapse."

The man in the black suit smirked.

"And what if we choose to keep things as they are?"

The Crystal Glass Man's surface darkened, reflecting the greed in their eyes.

"Then you will watch your empire fall. Not by our hands, but by the weight of your own choices."

The Phoenix of Love's voice was steady.

"You cannot fight truth forever. The world is waking up. The people will not remain silent much longer."

The council members shifted in their seats. Some were afraid. Others remained defiant.

The man in the black suit sat back, smirking.

"Let them rise. We have armies. We have influence. And most of all, we have all who are afraid on our side."

The Pearl of Wisdom pulsed once more, this time with sorrow.

"Then you have chosen your path."

The farmer sighed.

"Come, let's go. We have done what we came to do."

The team turned and walked out of the Tower of Wealth, leaving the council behind.

As they stepped outside, the sun was setting. The city glowed beneath them—rich and poor, powerful and powerless, standing side by side.

The Phoenix of Love gazed at the horizon.

"They will not change willingly. That means we must prepare for what comes next."

The Crystal Glass Man nodded.

"If they will not give power back to the people, then the people must reclaim it themselves."

The Pearl of Wisdom pulsed with determination.

"Then it is time to awaken the world."

Points for discussion on what this chapter accomplishes:

1. Confirms the Resistance of the Wealthy – The leaders refuse to change.

2. Foreshadows a Larger Movement – The people must now be awakened.

3. Establishes the Next Conflict – The ruling class will try to suppress the truth.

4. Builds Momentum for the Revolution – The world is on the verge of transformation.

Chapter Twelve: The Awakening—Bringing Truth to the People

The team stood outside the Tower of Wealth, watching the city below. The sky darkened, but the streets were alive with movement—workers returning home, merchants counting their earnings, and children playing among the shadows of skyscrapers.

The Pearl of Wisdom pulsed with determination.

"The rulers have chosen greed over justice. Now, it is time to awaken the people."

The Phoenix of Love nodded.

"But how? Many do not even realise they are trapped in a system designed to keep them powerless."

The Crystal Glass Man's surface shimmered.

"We must give them the truth. And for that, we need allies."

Just then, a gentle hum filled the air, growing louder by the second.

A golden swarm of bees appeared, their leader—a powerful, radiant Bee—landing gracefully before the group.

The Bee: The Power of Cooperation

The Bee studied the Pearl of Wisdom.

"You call for change, but no great change happens alone."

The farmer tilted his head.

"You mean we need more than just words?"

The Bee nodded.

"A single bee cannot sustain a hive. It is through unity, through thousands working as one, that true prosperity is built. This is the lesson the world has forgotten."

The Pearl of Wisdom pulsed in agreement.

"Then help us. Teach the people that wealth is not in gold, but in service to one another."

The Bee's wings buzzed with energy.

"Then we will spread the message."

And with that, the golden swarm dispersed into the city, whispering the truth into the ears of merchants, farmers, and workers alike.

A new consciousness began to stir.

The Dragonfly: Cutting Through the Illusions

As the message of unity spread, a flash of blue streaked across the sky.

A sharp-eyed Dragonfly hovered before the team, its wings shimmering with light.

The Phoenix of Love smiled.

"I was hoping you would come."

The Dragonfly's voice was swift and direct.

"I see what others ignore. The truth has been buried under layers of deception, but I can uncover it."

The farmer nodded.

"Then tell us—what is hidden?"

The Dragonfly's wings flickered, and suddenly, visions filled the air—secret meetings, corrupt deals, and powerful figures working to silence those who sought justice.

"The rulers are not only hoarding wealth," the Dragonfly said.

"They are manipulating information, keeping people blind to their own power."

Here I would like to introduce the strengths of the Dragonfly, who makes an integral part of our team.

The story of how the Dragonfly character came into existence

A shimmer of iridescent wings caught the light as the Dragonfly hovered above the group. Its multifaceted eyes, gleaming like tiny prisms, took in everything—not just what was in front of it, but the entire landscape, in a 360-degree panorama that no other creature could match.

The Phoenix of Love smiled knowingly.

"I was hoping you would come."

The Dragonfly spoke in a voice both swift and precise, each word landing with intention.

"I see what others ignore. The truth is often buried under layers of illusion, but my eyes cut through deception like a blade of light."

With a flick of its wings, the air shimmered around them, revealing glimpses of unseen forces at play—whispered meetings in darkened corridors, misdirection planted to lead others astray, and long-forgotten truths waiting to surface. The Dragonfly did not speculate or assume; it observed, dissected, and presented facts as they were.

Scientific Significance: The Ultimate Observer

The Dragonfly was no ordinary messenger. In nature, it was one of the most efficient hunters, its brain processing images faster than almost any other insect, predicting movement before its prey could react. It was capable of seeing in nearly every direction at once, its compound eyes composed of over 30,000 tiny lenses—a natural marvel of perception.

Much like the mind of a seasoned investigative journalist, it could track patterns, detect anomalies, and separate fact from fiction. Just as a dragonfly in the wild uses its sharp vision to locate mosquitoes in flight, this one could pinpoint misinformation and deception before they could cause harm.

Cultural Symbolism: Wisdom, Transformation, and Truth

In many cultures, the dragonfly is a symbol of transformation and enlightenment. In Japan, it represents victory and agility; in Native American traditions, it is the bringer of wisdom; and in some legends, it is a guardian of secrets, revealing only to those ready to see.

For the Chickpea and his team, the dragonfly was not merely a companion; it was a beacon of clarity, an unwavering guide that could navigate the fog of confusion and cut through distraction.

This is how this cultural symbolism is seen by the other characters:

The Crystal Glass Man admired its clarity, seeing it as a reflection of purity and truth.

The Phoenix of Love welcomed its insight, knowing that passion alone was not enough—wisdom was needed to direct that fire.

Borboleta, the Blue Butterfly, found inspiration in its ability to hover between realms of illusion and truth, much like the way she herself guided others through transformation.

Fidélis, the Australian Shepherd, sensed in the dragonfly a kindred spirit—both were guardians, one with eyes on the world, the other with ears tuned to danger.

Like a journalist in my wife's side of the family, always devoted to uncovering the full story, the dragonfly's greatest skill is contextual vision. It does not just capture fragments of information; it pieces together the puzzle, recognizing patterns that others may have missed. It could hover in place, much like a reporter holding steady against waves of misinformation. It could dart forward with speed, much like the sharp instincts of a journalist who knows when to press further. It could move in all directions, representing a mind that scans across history, present events, and hidden networks, forming a story with full perspective.

The team is discussing how the drone will operate and what it will be used for.

Just as the inventor adjusted the drone's final settings, a flicker of motion caught their eyes. A shimmering dragonfly hovered above the workbench, its delicate wings moving faster than the eye could follow.

The Chickpea gasped, "Who are you?"

The dragonfly landed on the drone, its many-faceted eyes glowing with an intense light.

"I am the Seer of Patterns," the dragonfly responded. "Where others see chaos, I see connections. Where others see obstacles, I see the pathways forward."

The Crystal Glass Man nodded, "You are the eye that perceives beyond what is obvious."

The Phoenix of Love smiled, "You move with purpose, neither swayed by distraction nor misled by illusions."

The Australian Shepherd sniffed the air and wagged his tail, "I trust him. His sight is different from mine, but his instincts are sharp."

Borboleta fluttered next to him, "We both move with the wind, but you—your wings are like needles, cutting through confusion."

The dragonfly's wings shimmered. "Indeed. In the world of the unseen, the smallest shift of movement tells the greatest story. You will need me, for the path ahead is filled with veiled truths and unseen dangers."

The Chickpea beamed, "Then you're part of our team."

The dragonfly nodded, "And I will help you see beyond the surface, discern the patterns hidden in the shadows, and navigate the turbulence ahead."

The inventor grinned, adjusting the drone's sensors, "Then it looks like our drone just got a second pair of eyes."

The Crystal Glass Man's face darkened, "Then we must reveal the truth."

The dragonfly's eyes gleamed, "I will carry your message where their lies cannot reach."

And with that, the dragonfly took flight, weaving through the city, cutting through illusion after illusion.

The American Eagle: Strength and Justice

As the movement began to stir, a powerful shadow passed over the city.

A majestic American Eagle soared above, landing on a high tower overlooking the people.

The farmer looked up in awe, "The guardian of justice has arrived."

The eagle's golden eyes surveyed the city below, "A nation is not measured by its riches, but by the strength of its people. The powerful have grown weak with greed, but the people—they are waking up."

The Pearl of Wisdom pulsed, "Then help us. Stand with us as we break the chains of economic warfare."

The eagle spread its mighty wings, "Justice is not given—it is claimed. The time has come for action."

The Phoenix of Love burned brighter, "Then let us rise together."

And as the eagle soared over the city, its cry rang out—a call to all those ready to reclaim their future.

.

The Ninth Character is Chosen – The Bee Returns and Joins the Team

(Ants were not mentioned prior to this)

The eight characters gathered in a sacred circle, each bringing their wisdom, experience, and energy, and the bee stepped in to join, humming softly. This was no ordinary meeting—this was a Bahá'í consultation, where every voice mattered, is attentively heard, and unity, not opinion, would guide the final decision. Bahá'í consultation is unique because it is spiritual, centres on unity, seeks the truth, is free of ego, and collective in decision-making. It emphasises detachment, humility, harmony, and the pursuit of truth over personal opinions.

The Phoenix of Love began, "We are here to choose our ninth and final member. Our circle is strong, but it is incomplete. We need a force that embodies service, discipline, and selflessness."

Borboleta fluttered above the gathering, "I have observed two extraordinary creatures. The ant, whose strength lies in its perseverance and teamwork, and the bee, who tirelessly serves its own kind, ensures the flourishing of life in other species."

The Australian Shepherd tilted his head, ever watchful, "Both creatures exemplify unity and dedication. The ants move in formation, driven by an unyielding purpose. The bees, however, bring something more—a deep sense of harmony, a natural rhythm of service that extends beyond their own kind."

The Pearl of Wisdom, always the seeker of truth, pondered aloud, "The ant builds, but the bee nourishes. The ant follows, but the bee communicates through dance. The ant organises, but the bee pollinates—giving life to others."

The Crystal Glass Man nodded, "Service is at the heart of our mission. The bee does not work for itself alone. It gives freely, ensuring that fields bloom, trees bear fruit, and flowers spread their beauty. Its labour is selfless, and its reward is in the flourishing of all."

The dragonfly, ever the observer of truth, circled above, "The bee's knowledge is vast. It navigates using the sun, speaks through movement, and builds with precision. In it, I see a guide for our own path—serving not just with effort, but with wisdom."

A hush fell over the group. Then, the once Chickpea, now transformed into the Pearl of Wisdom, spoke the words that sealed the decision: "The bees are a sign of divine order. They serve the greater good, work in unity, and create abundance wherever they go. If we must choose, let it be the bee."

The Phoenix of Love looked around the circle, meeting each pair of eyes, "Do we have unity?"

One by one, each character voiced their agreement. The vote was unanimous: the bee was to be the ninth and final member of their team.

A soft hum filled the air as the bee, golden and radiant, descended from the sky. It landed gently in their midst, its wings shimmering with an unseen light.

"I have always been here," the bee said with a knowing smile, "Waiting for you to be ready."

The Pearl of Wisdom bowed, "Then let us walk together. There is much to build."

And so, the nine were complete, their circle of unity unbroken, their mission fortified by the wisdom of consultation. Together, they would fulfil their intended purpose, create a world of service, promote learning, and foster a global transformation—one step, one flight, one act of love at a time.

The Awakening Begins

With the Bees spreading the message of unity, the Dragonfly exposing the truths held back for the right timing, and the Eagle leading the charge for justice, the people began to stir.

They questioned. They challenged. The people rose; the youth and children soared.

The streets, once filled with silent struggle, became alive with harmonious singing voices.

The Pearl of Wisdom hovered in the air, watching the change unfold.

"This is only the beginning."

The Crystal Glass Man's surface glowed. "The rulers will not sit idly by. They will resist."

The Phoenix of Love's wings burned bright. "Then let them. The fire of transformation has already begun."

The farmer took a deep breath, looking at the city that was waking up.

"Let the truth be known."

And with that, the world began to change.

Points for discussion on what this chapter accomplishes:

1. Introduces the Bee – Spreading the message of unity and cooperation.

2. Introduces the Dragonfly – Exposing hidden truths and deceptions.

3. Introduces the American Eagle – Symbolising leadership, justice, and action.

4. Begins the Awakening – The people start questioning and rising up.

5. Foreshadows Conflict – The rulers will not give up their power without a fight.

Chapter Thirteen: The Clash—The Battle for the Future Begins

The city was no longer silent.

The streets, once filled with quiet struggle, now pulsed with energy. Workers, merchants, and families gathered in the squares, listening to the words carried by the Bees, seeing the hidden truths revealed by the Dragonfly, and feeling the strength of the Eagle soaring above.

The awakening had begun.

But the rulers of the Tower of Wealth had been watching.

And they would not surrender their power without a fight.

The Council's Response

Deep inside the Tower of Wealth, the council gathered once more.

The man in the black suit stood at the head of the table, his face dark with fury.

"The people are stirring. The streets are no longer quiet. They are questioning. They are resisting."

A woman in pearls scowled. "We control everything—banks, industries, information. How can a handful of talking creatures and a glowing pearl cause this much disruption?"

A grey-haired strategist leaned forward. "Because they are not just talking. They are offering the people something we never could—hope."

The man in the black suit's fist tightened. "Then we must remind them who holds the real power."

A new plan was set in motion.

Within hours, news channels spread fear, accusing the movement of chaos and rebellion. Banks imposed sudden restrictions, making it harder for the people to access their own wealth. Police forces were deployed into the streets, ordered to silence the voices of the common people rising in protest. The rulers were striking back.

The Streets Erupt

The farmer and his team stood in the city square, watching as armoured forces moved in.

The Australian Shepherd growled with a warning bark. "They are trying to crush the movement before it spreads further."

The Crystal Glass Man's surface darkened and he said, "Fear is their weapon. They will try to turn the people against us."

The Pearl of Wisdom pulsed with determination, addressing the team. "Then we must remind the people that true power does not come from towers of gold, but from those who stand together."

The Phoenix of Love's wings blazed with light and spoke, "Then let us stand up for ourselves."

As the soldiers marched forward, the people did not flee. Instead, they held their ground. The Bee flew above, calling out to the workers and said, "You built this city with your hands! You created the wealth they hoard! Without you, their empire is nothing!"

The Dragonfly darted between the soldiers, whispering truths on building the new order.

"The real danger is not in those who question the old ways, but in those who silence them and stay stagnant."

The American Eagle soared above, its cry ringing through the air:

"A nation built on fear will crumble! A nation built on justice will rise!"

The people, once afraid, now stood tall.

The rulers had power, but the people now had an awakened conscience and were cautious.

The Breaking Point

The man in the black suit watched from the Tower of Wealth, his jaw clenched.

"They are not afraid anymore," one of his advisers muttered.

The man turned sharply and said, "Then we will make them afraid."

He picked up a phone.

Within moments, the skies darkened—not with storm clouds, but with drones, surveillance, and reinforcements.

A final message echoed through the city's loudspeakers:

"Return to your homes. Obey, and you will be safe. Resist, and you will suffer."

A tense silence fell.

Then the Pearl of Wisdom rose into the air with his helicopter and, through his built-in megaphone, spoke one final truth:

"A system built on fear will always fear the truth. But fear cannot rule forever."

The Phoenix of Love's wings blazed and added, "What will you choose—obedience to fear, or freedom through unity?"

A heartbeat passed. Then—one by one—the people stepped forward, not as rebels, not as enemies, but as citizens reclaiming their world.

The clash was no longer between rulers and rebels.

It was between truth and deception. And truth had finally risen.

Points for discussion on what this chapter accomplishes:

1. Shows the rulers' counterattack – Fear, suppression, and economic control.
2. Highlights the people's response – Courage, unity, and resistance to fear.

3. Demonstrates the power of wisdom – The team uses knowledge, not violence, to counter oppression.

4. Sets up the final confrontation – The old system is crumbling, but will the rulers surrender?

Chapter Fourteen: The Fall of the Tower—A New Era Begins

The streets of the city stood still.

The people had risen, not with weapons but with truth, not in rage but in quiet power.

And thus began what history would later call the fall of the Tower.

But it was not an ending. It was the beginning of something greater.

The rulers of the Tower of Wealth watched from their high windows, seeing the crowds standing firm below.

The man in the black suit clenched his jaw and said, "They should be afraid, but they aren't."

They were waiting—not for revenge, not for destruction—but for a resolution that did not demand blood, only justice.

The Power of Timing

The Crystal Glass Man turned to the Pearl of Wisdom and said, "Justice is calling, but it is not yet time to strike. If we force change too soon, we risk losing what we have built."

The Phoenix of Love nodded, commenting wisely, "A fire that burns too hot consumes even the innocent. We must hold steady."

The Bee hovered in the air, saying, "The hive survives not by attacking, but by knowing when to act."

The Dragonfly whispered, "For everything in nature, we see the right time for maturity, when there is more receptivity for truth, love, and unity—that's what is meant by 'The Power of Timing.' The truth has already been revealed. Let it settle. Let it take root."

As the American Eagle circled above, he stated, "A wise leader knows that victory does not come from crushing the enemy, but from showing them a better way."

As the Pearl of Wisdom pulsed, he pointed out, "Then we do not force justice today. We plant it. And in the right time, it will grow, and the new society will emerge."

A Moment of Surrender

Inside the Tower of Wealth, the rulers saw the shift.

They had expected anger, uprising, demand for retribution.

But the people below did not cry for revenge.

They stood in unity.

And suddenly, the power the rulers had always wielded—the power of fear—was gone.

The man in the black suit sat down slowly. He had spent his life controlling people with wealth and fear.

Now, neither could hold them.

One of the council members whispered, "What do we do now?"

For the first time, there was no answer, only silence.

The Dragonfly reappeared and said, "The maturity of mankind and the light of unity have been enkindled. Now we see the beginning of the silent affirmation, incandescence, and a 'Moment of Surrender' of the Council of the Wealthy."

The Tower had not fallen by force. It had fallen because no one believed in it anymore.

The Beginning of a New Era

The Pearl of Wisdom turned to the people and declared,

"Today, we do not tear down. We do not punish. We do not seek revenge. We build."

The Phoenix of Love's wings flickered softly. She stated,

"Justice will come, not through anger, but through renewal."

The American Eagle landed beside the Pearl and said,

"And in time, even those who ruled will see that true power does not lie in gold, but in service."

A hush fell over the crowd.

The farmer placed a hand over his heart.

"Then let today mark not the fall of an empire, but the rise of a new world."

The people cheered—not in triumph, but in hope.

A new economy would be built, a new system would emerge—not by war, not by revenge, but by wisdom, patience, and unity.

Points for discussion on what this chapter accomplishes:

1. Shows restraint in justice—Choosing peace over vengeance.
2. Demonstrates the power of patience—Change comes at the right time, not by force.
3. Reveals the true fall of the rulers—Not through destruction, but through irrelevance.
4. Sets up a new beginning—A world rebuilt on service, not greed.

The Dawn of a New Civilization

The city, once ruled by fear, now stood on the edge of something new—building a new society.

The Tower of Wealth remained standing, but its power had dissolved. No soldiers patrolled the streets. No leaders issued commands.

Instead, the people gathered—not in defiance, but in unity.

A new question filled the air, "What now?"

As the Pearl of Wisdom hovered above the city square, he said, "Now, we build."

A Vision for the Future

The Phoenix of Love looked to the horizon. "But first, we must decide what kind of a world we wish to create."

The American Eagle soared overhead, saying, "One built not on power, but on justice."

The Crystal Glass Man's surface shimmered as he pointed out, "Not on wealth, but on balance."

The Bee landed on the farmer's shoulder and added, "Not on control, but on cooperation."

The Dragonfly's wings flickered and said, "Not on deception, but on truth."

The farmer stepped forward.

"Then let us lay the foundation—not with gold, but with trust; not with walls, but with knowledge."

The First Steps

The people divided into groups by purpose instead of class or wealth.

◆ Builders began restoring homes and roads—this time, for everyone, not just for the elite.

◆ Farmers gathered to plan sustainable ways to feed the people.

◆ Teachers stepped forward to share knowledge freely, no longer restricted by wealth.

◆ Healers opened their doors to all, seeing health as a right, not a privilege.

◆ Artists, musicians, and thinkers came together to create not for profit, but for joy.

The old economy had crumbled, but in its place, something new and much fairer was rising.

The Pearl's Final Message

The Pearl of Wisdom pulsed with warmth through the megaphone and said, "This is only the beginning. The road ahead will not always be easy. There will be struggles, and there will be trials." But now, he said, addressing the people, "You are not powerless—you never were."

The Phoenix of Love's wings glowed softly and, as she joined in, said emphatically, "The greatest civilizations are not built in a day, but in the hearts of those who refuse to give up on justice."

The American Eagle gazed at the people and added, "And justice, once planted, cannot be uprooted."

The farmer placed his hand on his heart, declaring, "The good things are going to happen. They won't happen overnight—it's a process. Then let this be the first dawn of many."

As the sun rose over the horizon, the world took its first breath as something new—something with a new order and new entity; a civilization not built on greed but on wisdom, not ruled by fear but by unity, not driven by profit but by purpose: a world where everyone had a place, a world where true prosperity had finally begun.

As the first rays of dawn broke over the horizon, a delicate blue butterfly danced in the golden light. The Chickpea, now changed, now whole, watched in awe as Borboleta reappeared and landed gently on his shoulder.

"You have grown," she said with a knowing smile. "But remember—transformation is not a single moment. It is a journey without end."

With that, she spread her wings and lifted into the sky, her presence a promise that renewal would always come to those who sought it.

Points for discussion on what this chapter accomplishes:

1. Establishes the new civilisation—built on wisdom, justice, cooperation, and purpose.
2. Shows the first steps of rebuilding—people working together freely, without oppression.
3. Delivers the Pearl's final message—change is never-ending; the journey must continue.
4. Sets up a larger mission—the team's wisdom must reach the rest of the world.

Epilogue: The Journey Continues

The book is not coaching that peace is established, but that we are at the dawn of a New Era.

As the people worked, the team stood together—watching carefully, knowing their mission was not yet complete.

The Crystal Glass Man turned to the Pearl of Wisdom and said, "You have given them the light. But there are still many who have yet to see it."

The Phoenix of Love nodded, responding, "We must carry this message beyond these lands—to the farthest corners of the world."

The Dragonfly hovered. "There are still shadows to illuminate."

While the Bee's wings hummed, he added, "Still hives to build."

The American Eagle stretched its wings and further added, "Still justice to deliver."

The Pearl of Wisdom pulsed one last time, looking at the world they had helped shape. "Then let us go forward—not as rulers, not as conquerors, but as guides," he suggested.

And as the team took flight, leaving behind a world forever changed, a new—much brighter—story began. A story of hope, of balance, of the wisdom that would continue to shape the future, because transformation.

The Council of Nine: A Conversation on the Nine Principles of ITOE – The Interface Theory of Organizational Energy

ITOE is a theory the Author created about Organizational Energy and stages of change and transformation that apply to organizations, groups, as well as individuals.

(The following is Nokhodee, now the Pearl of Wisdom, interacting with his eight companions as a team to explain ITOE, which was created by his spiritual father, in order to foster virtues, create sustainable change, and prepare those involved for a life of service.)

Some last words by the Pearl of Wisdom (Nokhodee) to the team:

"My dear friends, we have gathered today not only as a team, but we are a family of wisdom, courage, and service. Each of us brings something special, and together, we can inspire children, guide the youth, and energize the world."

☐ When Pearl of Wisdom speaks:

🫧 **Pearl of Wisdom:** "We must ensure that all principles work together like a pearl forming layer by layer. Only then can we create a future filled with harmony and wisdom."

☐ When Crystal Glass Man speaks:

💎 **Crystal Glass Man:** "Just as glass reflects all colors of the rainbow, we must reflect all perspectives to bring true unity among people."

📖 When Phoenix of Love speaks:

🔥 **Phoenix of Love:** "Out of hardship, we rise! We must help children understand that every challenge strengthens their spirit."

📖 When Dragonfly speaks:

🦗 **Dragonfly:** "Through my 360-degree vision, I can see past illusions. Truth-seeking is essential for clarity and wisdom."

But before we move forward, let us reflect on the nine principles of ITOE. Why are they so important? And what do we each need to improve on to truly serve humanity?" Nokhodee continued, "Einstein discovered a physical theory that describes how the merest atoms are the source of immense energy., by the same token, transformation with humans and organizations energy need a theory too. Now we will explore a theory that helps us to bring about a sustainable and lasting change – to serve the world."

The 9 Principles of ITOE:

1st Principle: Routines & Healthy Habits

(Building strong foundations through daily practice and discipline.)

🟢 Crystal Glass Man:

"Everything starts with a good habit! Just like how glass needs careful shaping before it becomes strong, children need good routines—prayer, kindness, study, and service. With these I learned my crystal glows and shows all the colours of the rainbow."

🟠 Phoenix of Love:

"I agree! Love grows through small acts, repeated every day. We must practise patience, care, and resilience in our daily lives. How can we teach children to build these habits?"

🔵 Australian Shepherd:

"I can help with this! I guide and protect others. Good habits are like learning to follow the right path. If children see consistency in what we do, they will learn to trust, follow, and develop strong routines."

2nd Principle: Journaling & Self-Reflection

(Understanding ourselves and our progress.)

🔴 **Dragonfly:**

"As a truth-seeker, I know that writing things down helps us see clearly! Journaling helps children remember their lessons, emotions, and thoughts—just like how I use my big eyes to see everything from many angles."

🟡 **Bee:**

"Yes! In my hive, we record everything—where the best flowers are, how to make honey. If we didn't write things down, we'd forget where to go! Reflection helps children become more organised, wise, and grateful." In this way, through dancing, the bees show the team where to go and how to find the right flowers.

🔵 **Dolphin:**

"Reflection isn't just about words. It's about listening too! I use echolocation to understand my surroundings. We must help children reflect by asking questions and listening deeply to their hearts."

3rd Principle: Positioning & Perspective

(Understanding where we stand and what comes next.)

🦅 American Eagle:

"I see far and wide! Just like a bird that flies high, children must learn to look at their lives from a bigger perspective. Are they making the right choices? Where are they heading? We must teach them to aim for the highest goals."

🔥 Phoenix of Love:

"But balance is important too! It's not just about looking forward, but also looking inside, understanding where we are, and being content with each step."

4th Principle: Resilience & Overcoming Challenges

(Learning how to stand up after falling down.)

🦋 Borboleta:

"I started as a caterpillar. It was hard! But I transformed. Children must learn that challenges help them grow. Every difficulty is part of their journey to becoming something beautiful."

🐝 Bee:

"When it rains, I don't stop working. I dry my wings and keep going. We must teach children to face difficulties with courage. Together, we can overcome anything!"

5th Principle: Goal Setting & Vision for the Future

(Creating clear goals and working towards them.)

🔷 Pearl of Wisdom:

"A ship without direction is lost at sea. We must set goals, so we know where we're going. Our mission is to prepare children to serve, unite, and build a better world."

◆ Crystal Glass Man:

"Each goal is like a piece of glass being shaped by fire. It may take time, but with patience and vision, we can create something clear and beautiful."

6th Principle: Multi-Functionality & Adaptability

(Learning to do many things and work in harmony.)

🐬 Dolphin:

"I am playful, smart, and I love teamwork! Children must learn to be flexible, to adjust to change, and to work with others. This will help them solve problems and be creative!"

🔴 Dragonfly:

"Yes! We must learn to adapt to new situations. Just as I move swiftly in the air, children must learn to adjust to life's challenges without fear." I have 360° vision and I can see all around me, and I am tempted to do many things, as I often do, but I still focus on my main goal."

7th Principle: Learning & Teaching Others

(Gaining knowledge and sharing it with love.)

🔥 Phoenix of Love:

"Learning is a flame that never goes out. The more we learn, the more we can help others. Teaching what we learn makes the fire spread, lighting the way for others."

🐕 Australian Shepherd:

"I learn from my surroundings every day! Children should never stop learning, and they should help others learn too. That's how we grow as a community."

8th Principle: Process Balance – Attending to Every Principle with Care

(Ensuring each step in the journey of change is given proper attention)

🧭 Definition

The 8th Principle is about distributing your efforts evenly across all nine principles of ITOE. It's not enough to just focus on journalling (P2) or setting goals (P5)—you need to assess, adjust, and revisit every principle regularly. It's the harmony of process.

🍰 **Analogy:** Think of baking a cake—not just having the right ingredients, but following the right steps: mixing, resting, baking, cooling. Miss a step or rush one, and the cake fails.

🐝 **Bee:** "We bees don't just make honey—we clean, build, guard, and nurture. Just like a healthy hive, the process of change needs attention at every step. You can't say, 'I journalled, so I'm done!' You must check how you're doing, reset goals, and continue the cycle."

🐬 **Dolphin:** "In our pod, everyone plays a role—not just in swimming, but in teaching, feeding, and guiding. Skipping any of these harms the whole. The same with change: if you skip assessing your progress or fail to revisit your purpose, something vital is lost."

💎 **Pearl of Wisdom:** "Just like my layers formed over time, your transformation is a process. You might start with routines (P1), write them down (P2), but if you forget to reflect (P3) or redirect your goals (P5), the pearl remains unfinished. The 8th principle says: treat every step with respect."

9th Principle: Energy Balance – Choosing the Right Energy Mix for the Moment

(Harmonising physical, mental, emotional, and spiritual efforts based on life stage and context)

🔬 **Definition:** The 9th Principle focuses on using the correct proportion of energies—T1 (physical), T2 (mental), T3 (emotional), and T4 (spiritual)—at any given time. As individuals and organisations evolve, their energy needs shift.

🎂 **Analogy:** Flour, eggs, sugar, and milk—each is a vital energy. Some moments need more T1 (like financial or physical support), others more T4 (legacy, virtue, spiritual guidance). Balance means adjusting the mix based on what's being "baked."

🦅 **American Eagle:** "When I was younger, I needed strength—T1—and sharp thinking—T2. But now, as a mentor, I rely more on insight and values—T4. The winds of life shift, and so must our energy. A soaring flight needs balance—not too much weight on one wing."

🦋 **Borboleta:** "In the rainforest, I must drink deeply—T1—before I take flight. But when I glide above the trees, it's my joy, my purpose—T4—that keeps me going. Some days I need rest, others I dance in the wind. Life flows better when we mix our energies wisely."

Final Reflections: A Pledge for the Future

Pearl of Wisdom looked at his companions and smiled.

"My dear friends, we have reflected on what makes us strong. But now, we must each make a pledge—a promise to improve something in ourselves, so that we can help children better."

One by one, the companions made their promises:

- 🔮 **Crystal Glass Man:** "I will work on bringing more people together, helping them see the beauty in diversity."

- 🔥 **Phoenix of Love:** "I will help children be strong even when times are tough."

- 🦋 **Borboleta:** "I will remind children that they can transform, no matter where they start."

- 🐸 **Dragonfly:** "I will help children see the truth and think clearly."

- 🐕 **Australian Shepherd:** "I will protect those who feel alone and forgotten."

- 🦅 **American Eagle:** "I will help children dream big and aim high."

- 🐬 **Dolphin:** "I will teach children to work together with joy."

- 🐝 **Bee:** "I will remind everyone that we are stronger when we serve together."

- 🦪 **Pearl of Wisdom:** "I will guide us all to stay true to our purpose—to bring love, knowledge, and unity to the world."

Then, they all joined hands, wings, paws, and antennae in unity. A new chapter was beginning—not just for them, but for the world.

Character Symbols Key

✅ 🦪 **Pearl of Wisdom (Nokhodee)** → Represents wisdom emerging through trials.

✅ 🔮 **Crystal Glass Man (CGM)** → Symbolises transparency, clarity, and unity.

✅ 🔥 **Phoenix of Love** → Represents resilience, renewal, and passion.

✅ 🦋 **Borboleta (Blue Butterfly)** → Symbolises transformation and the beauty of change.

✅ 🐕 **Australian Shepherd** → Represents loyalty, guidance, and protection.

✅ 🦅 **American Eagle** → Symbolises vision, leadership, and courage.

✅ 🐬 **Dolphin** → Represents intelligence, communication, and teamwork.

✅ 🐝 **Bee** → Symbolises hard work, community, and service.

✅ 🦗 **Dragonfly** → Represents truth-seeking, clarity, and adaptability.

A Final Thought

The book has now come full circle, showing that true transformation is not a destination, but an ongoing journey.

Author's Note: A Reflection on Transformation

Dear Reader,

This journey began with a simple idea—a chickpea longing for transformation—and grew into a story of wisdom, justice, and the search for a better world.

But this is more than a story.

It is a vision, a call to action, a reminder that change does not come from the powerful; it comes from those who dare to believe in something greater.

We live in a world where economic warfare, division, and deception often cloud our vision. Yet, just like the characters in this book, we have the ability to see through the illusions, uncover the truth, and reshape our future.

Each of us carries a Pearl of Wisdom within us—the potential to uplift, to serve, to guide, and to build.

The path forward is not always easy. Sometimes, justice must wait for the right moment. Sometimes, the most powerful action is patience, resilience, and unity.

But one thing is certain: the world is ready for transformation, and that transformation begins with you.

May you always seek truth.

May you always serve with love.

And may you always have the courage to rise.

With gratitude,

Shah

The Final Message: Transformation is for the World

The Pearl of Wisdom understands that transformation never ends with the self.

He turns to his companions and says:

"We were never meant to walk this journey alone. Now, together, we will serve."

And with that, the journey is complete.

Yet, it is also just beginning.

Because true transformation is not a destination—it is a way of being, a life of service, and a commitment to always grow, always uplift, and always shine.

About the Author

Shahrokh Pezeshk is an Iranian-born author, educator, and international consultant in change leadership. With decades of experience working across Brazil, the United States, and Australia, he has helped governments, schools, businesses, and communities navigate complex transformation processes. This book blends his professional expertise with his deep spiritual curiosity—offering a story that speaks to the inner child in all of us and lays the foundation for building a new civilization rooted in unity, service, and moral leadership.

Whether you are a child searching for wonder, a parent seeking values-based stories, or a leader guiding others through change, this book offers a lantern of light in uncertain times. It reminds us that, like the Chickpea, our smallest beginnings can lead to the greatest transformations.

www.ingramcontent.com/pod-product-compliance
Lightning Source LLC
Chambersburg PA
CBHW041613220426
43670CB00001B/7